THE
SECRET OF MARY CELESTE

The Secret
of
Mary Celeste

and other sea fare

By Gershom Bradford

Illustrations by Harold Durand White

LONDON
W. FOULSHAM & CO. LTD.
NEW YORK - TORONTO - CAPE TOWN - SYDNEY

W. FOULSHAM & CO. Ltd.
Yeovil Road Slough Bucks, England

COPYRIGHT © 1966 By BARRE PUBLISHING CO.
Library of Congress Catalog Card Number 66-26950
Made and Printed in Great Britain
by Willmer Brothers Limited, Birkenhead

To
MAMIE

who for so many years has been . . .
"Like that star on starry nights,
    The seaman singles from the sky,
To steer his bark forever by."

ACKNOWLEDGMENTS

My appreciation is extended to those friends who have furnished me information connected with these episodes. I thank those editors who have kindly given me permission to use material which I have previously contributed to their magazines:

The American Neptune: The Secret of Mary Celeste is a drastic revision of Mary Celeste, No, Not Again, previously published.

On a Lee Shore.

The Rudder: The Sloop Granite.

Yachting: The Cold Call of Duty and The Reader of the Sky. The latter is a revision of The Sky Reader.

G.B.

TO THE READER

When I was a boy of about 9 years, my father took me along to visit an old shipowner. Most of the call was devoted to the mystery of the brigantine Mary Celeste, which had been found singularly abandoned some 15 years before. The old gentleman told a graphic tale which made a deep impression on my young mind.

Through all the intervening years I have seen innumerable articles and perhaps five books on the subject. The best of these, and fairly recent is, *The Mary Celeste*: *The Odyssey of an Abandoned Ship* by Charles Edey Fay.

My friend Francis E. Cross, loaned me this fine book and while studying it, a practical solution flashed in my mind. Returning the book I told the Captain that a waterspout had caused the brigantine's troubles. He thoughtfully looked out the window and said, "I think you have an idea there." He said that he had seen two waterspouts in the North Atlantic and was glad that he was not in a sailing vessel.

In my years in the Hydrographic Office I had seen many reports of waterspouts and their damage to ships, especially sailing craft. With this incentive I wrote an article for The American Neptune, which received so much favourable comment among naval officers and shipmasters, that I have been encouraged to revise, augment and analyse some of the solutions that have appeared from time to time.

Admittedly the explanations are somewhat technical and drawn out. If they prove tedious, skip over them lightly. To relax the reader after the complexities presented by this intriguing brig, I have provided a group of sailor involvements that may help to while away a leisure hour. All these I have collected through the years spent among seamen. Yes, many years, extending back to 1898 and beyond.

In my youth aboard ship I clearly recall the night watches on the forecastle head. Rising high aloft the swelling canvas weaved fascinating shadows among the stars. Over the rail below was the onward surge of the bow wave. Ahead, the bowsprit was pointing to the years and hopes downwind. There, I now realize, was the post of youth, there the "young man could see visions."

The ways of the sailor and the beauty of the ships became my enthusiasms. Sixty-five years have dropped astern since I used to watch the bowsprit pointing to the future. Now I feel myself, as it were, standing at the taffrail. Astern spreads the streaming, bubbling wake of memory. I am reminded of the sailors and the ships and of the things I have seen and heard and felt. It is here that an "old man can dream dreams."

Contents

XXXXXXXXXXXXXXXXXXXXXXXXXXXXXXXXXXXXXXX

Illustrations

PART I

The
Secret of Mary Celeste

The Secret of Mary Celeste

"ABANDONED at sea!" That was a haunting phrase found in the columns of shipping intelligence of the past. It often suggested some delusive fear leading to a premature abandonment of the ship, or worse, mutiny, barratry or murder. Aboard the derelict *Mary Celeste* there was mystery. No evidence of crime has been revealed, yet fore and aft the crew had left a hasty and frightened trail. For 90 years and more the ample implications have spurred countless literary sleuths to put their solutions in the record—many of these getting beyond the control of reason. There always seems to be a place for another presentation.

Why, how and when did her crew leave her? Those are the perennial questions that comprise the secret of that pretty little brigantine. So another attempt will be made to answer them, perhaps, of necessity a bit technical here and there. Yet, it must be done in a seamanly manner, analyzing and weighing the known facts carefully, hoping thereby to gain support for the conclusions that are here advanced. Only natural phenomena will be employed and the ways of ships and sailors will be followed.

Perhaps it will be well to first become acquainted with *Mary Celeste* and her crew. To do this let us transport ourselves in fancy back to the year 1872 and first of November.

We are attracted to a little brigantine lying at a wharf in the East River, New York. She is about 100 feet long, 25 feet beam and measures 282 tons. The mate, Albert G. Richardson, a capable man from the State of Maine, is in charge, directing the loading and other ship's work. He is connected by marriage with the owner W. H. Winchester. Captain Benjamin S. Briggs comes and goes about the ship's business. He hails from Marion, Massachusetts, and is well known as a man of wide experience and excellent reputation.

As sailing day approaches he arrives one morning with his wife Sarah and little Sophia only two years old; they are going to make the voyage with him. Among the baggage they bring is a melodian, as they hope to have some "sings" to brighten the dog watches. On November 4 the captain signs on the crew; they are, besides Mr. Richardson, second mate Edward Gillings; cook, Edward W. Head; and four German sailors. Two of these are brothers, Lorenzen, by name; they came from the North Friesian Islands, in the North Sea, as did Arian Martens. These men have wives and relatives at home and there is testimony that they are home-loving, not of a type to be troublesome aboard ship. Of the fourth man Gottschalk, little is known, but as his name is familiar among those islands he too may have hailed from there. At least Captain Briggs after sizing up his crew is satified that he has a "peaceful lot."

At last the final barrel of the cargo, which is alcohol, is lowered to the hold and is stowed; the mate now turns his attention to the important duty of battening down the main hatch. It is perhaps, 10 feet square and is vulnerable should a heavy sea be shipped. Two, or perhaps four, sections of planks are placed in the hatchway, resting on a flange, which brings them flush with the top of the coaming; this is about a foot above the deck. Over these hatch covers are stretched two or even three pieces of stout canvas (tarpaulins) and firmly pressed to the sides of the coaming by battens secured with wedges. The corners, dogs' ears, receive careful attention as they might be caught by a sea and the tarpaulins ripped off, in which case the wooden covers could easily become dislodged through buoyancy and water pour below.

After Mr. Richardson sees this main hatch secured to his satisfaction, he has the yawl, their only boat, about 18 feet long, placed upon it and lashed down. Normally this boat would be carried across the stern at the davits but somehow during the loading the longboat has been damaged and is left on the wharf. He next gives the fore hatch his attention; this is smaller, the cover being in one piece, and, except in rough weather, is not as securely battened down. It is necessary at times to ventilate the hold and access is needed to reach the lockers in the foreward part of the vessel.

Sailing day arrives with all the details and formalities completed and on November 5 1872 the *Mary Celeste* drops down the harbour, but finding the wind ahead, she anchors off Staten Island. On Thursday the 7th she sails for good. The course is laid, as it has been for years by all Mediterranean-bound vessels, to pass through the Azores Islands, their high peaks make good landmarks. The skippers use them to square up their longitude before setting the course for Cape St. Vincent, the European landfall of Gibraltar-bound vessels. On the run to the Azores the winds are mostly westerly providing the brigantine with favourable conditions.

During the leisure of this run is a good time for us to look about the vessel and note the deck and cabin arrangements. The fore hatch before mentioned, is forward of the foremast and immediately abaft this mast is the forward house; it is divided fore and aft amidships, the gally being to starboard with a scuttle hatch overhead; and to port, forward, is the forecastle with four bunks; abaft which is a cubby hole with a bunk. Then comes the main hatch with the boat on it and just forward of the mainmast is the ship's pump. Abaft the mainmast is the cabin house, riding about 18

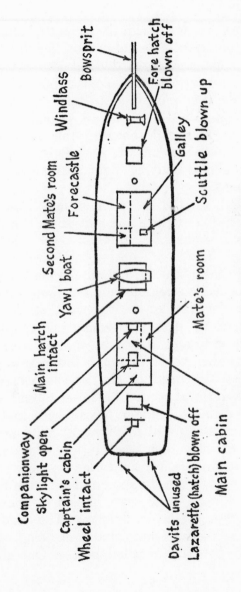

Companionway
Skylight open
Captain's cabin
Wheel intact

Davits unused
Lazarette (hatch) blown off
Main cabin

Main hatch intact

Yawl boat

Second Mate's room
Forecastle

Windlass

Bowsprit

Fore hatch blown off

Galley

Scuttle blown up

Mate's room

Mary Celeste - Deck Plan (Approximate)

B

inches above the deck, with the lazarette hatch and wheel at the stern. The cabin, reached by going down a companionway, is divided into two compartments; forward is the main cabin with the dining table; the pantry and W.C. are to port and the rooms of the mate and second mate to starboard. A bulkhead separates this main room from the captain's cabin aft. A skylight is located over the bulkhead giving light and air to both compartments.

So much for the deck, let us now look aloft for a description of the spars and sails. The *Mary Celeste* is a brigantine, therefore she has two masts, square-rigged on the fore and fore and aft on the mainmast. That is, forward, the mast is made up of three sections, the lowermast, then attached above this the topmast and above that the topgallant (t'gallant) mast, all forming one composite mast which is heavily stayed by shrouds, fore and back Spars called yards, cross this foremast at right angles; near the head of the lower-mast is the foreyard, a little above is the lower-topsail yard, again above this the upper topsail yard and still higher the t'gallant and royal yards. Sails, rectangular in shape have their heads (upper edges) made fast and when not in use, are furled on these yards; but when needed are dropped and set from them. The lower corners of each are hauled by sheets to the outer ends of the yard below. The yards, in order to trim the sails, are capable of being swung horizontally by tackles called braces. Out ahead,

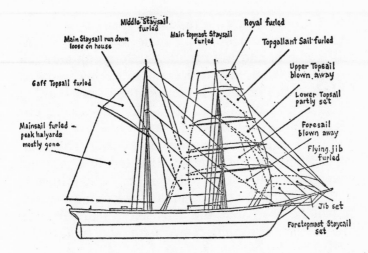

set from stays to the bowsprit and jib-boom are
three sails called head sails, nearest the mast is
the fore-topmast staysail, which is in effect a jib.
Then the jib, and outermost, the flying jib. On
the mainmast there is the usual so-called, schooner,
or fore and aft, rig, consisting of a mainsail with
the gaff topsail above it. Between the masts are two
or three staysails, something like jibs. This will
seem a long and technical description to some but
is necessary for an understanding of the points to
be made.

The *Celeste* makes the run to the Azores without notable incident and is among the islands on
November 24 with a strong and rising westerly
wind. Toward nightfall it reaches a moderate gale

and Captain Briggs, prudent seaman that he is, begins to shorten down.... The royal and "t'gansail" come in and are furled; the flying jib and gaff topsail are taken in and the mainsail is lowered and furled on the boom. This leaves the vessel running under a proper balance of sail for the strong fair wind which is blowing two or three points (22°-23°) on the starboard (right) quarter. The gaining strength of the wind is reflected in the speed which has been 8 knots but at 8 p.m., when the gale is at its height she picked up and is logging 9 knots. It will be seen that the sails left set are the jib, fore-topmast staysail, (*both with sheets fast for starboard tack*) the square foresail, upper and lower topsails, perhaps the main staysail.

Captain Briggs is often on deck during this dark and rainy night and it really does rain! Toward morning he is especially alert, for ahead is the island of Santa Maria; there are no lighthouses (1872) to warn him of its presence. At 5 a.m. the western end of the island is sighted and during the early morning the vessel runs along off its northern side, reaching the eastern point at 8 a.m., November 25 by civil date. The officer on watch takes a bearing and picking up the log slate, that is always at hand, enters an historic item: "Eastern Point bears SSW, 6 miles distant." Theses are the last written or spoken words from any member of the crew.

We have now reached a point in following what is known to have occurred aboard the *Mary*

Celeste and where we must transfer our attention temporarily to another vessel back in New York: It is again early in November and we make the acquaintance of the Nova Scotian brigantine *Dei Gratia*, Captain David R. Morehouse. She too, is loading for the Mediterranean and sails on the 12th, five days after the *Celeste*. She also follows more or less the usual route. The days pass without incident, the winds are largely westerly and good progress is made. Her course is considerably northward of Santa Maria and passing that Island, out of sight to the southward, the little *Dei Gratia* is well on her way to Gibraltar.

It is the quiet afternoon of December 4, 1872 on the Atlantic eastward of the Azores—near Lat. 38° 20' N.,—Lg 17° 15' W. The wind is light, northerly. The *Dei Gratia* with all sails set, is making a lazy 4 knots on her course. Captain Morehouse and second mate Wright are on deck; Mate Oliver Deveau is in his bunk. It is about 2 p.m. Someone sights a sail. This is always a break in shipboard monotony; but here the captain and second mate Wright, lowering their glasses, seem unusually aroused and puzzled; they call Mr. Deveau. The word passes forward; all hands appear on deck. As the *Dei Gratia* draws nearer, they see that the stranger is a brigantine like themselves with only two head-sails set and the fore-lower-topsail hanging loose; she is heading westward. Obviously something is wrong. The afterguard decides to board her. A boat is launched, manned by Mr.

Deveau, Wright and a sailor. They pull across.
When within hailing distance the mate shouts:
    "Aboard the brig."
    There is no answer. No one is seen on deck.
They pull for the lee side passing under the stern,
and to their amazement read: "*Mary Celeste*, New
York." Mr. Deveau remembers that she sailed shortly before the *Dei Gratia*. The sailor tends the boat
while the mates climb aboard. Mr. Deveau's practiced and astonished eye makes a sweeping survey,
followed by a detail inspection; he satisfies himself
that there is no one on board. Aloft, he sees that
the fore-upper topsail and foresail have been blown

away; that the fore-lower-topsail has been ripped from the jackstay, (that is, its fastenings along the yard) but is held by the earings and sheets ("by the four corners"). The two headsails are intact and *trimmed for the starboard tack* (as on the evening of November 24). The running rigging is badly fouled up. The wheel aft, is found in good order but the compass has been knocked from its position on the cabin house and broken; the lazarette hatch is off, the cabin skylight is up.

In the cabin, on the table, is the log slate on which appears that last entry of 8 a.m. November 25, 1872, nine days before. Deveau reads the bearing and distance that she had passed Santa Maria's Eastern Point. The after (living) quarters are reasonably orderly but there are indications of water having been below and of a hasty departure; the bed in the master's cabin is not made; everything is damp and the clock on the bulkhead, between the main and master's cabin, is "spoilt by water," apparently from the open skylight.

Forward of the mainmast the ship's pump occupies Mr. Deveau's particular attention; a sounding rod is lying on the deck, indicating a last measurement of water in the hold. This pump has two wells or cylinders, one to port, and the other to starboard of 'midships. The upper boxes or valves work up and down alternately as the men work the brakes—the handles. By a singular omission, when this brigantine recently received a new spar deck, a vertical sounding pipe was not provided, so it was necessary to detach and withdraw one of the boxes from the cylinder in order to drop the sounding rod, a very awkward necessity should the vessel be leaking rapidly. And significantly, one of the boxes has been withdrawn from its cylinder and is lying there on the deck beside the pump. Mr. Deveau drops the sounding rod down the open well and finds only $3\frac{1}{2}$ feet in her; not bad for a vessel that has not been pumped for nine days.

The main hatch appears to be secure and well battened, but the boat, which, by the lashings, had evidently been secured there, is gone, and a removable section of the ship's rail abreast the hatch, is lying on the deck, no doubt removed to facilitate the launching of the boat.

The hatch over the galley is off and there is a foot of water swashing about within; interestingly there is no water in the port side which has no open hatch above or open door. The cook's pots, pans and dishes are washed and in their places.

The forward hatch is off. Mr. Deveau finds a "large quantity of water" in the 'tween decks; he discovers that the vessel is loaded with barrels of alcohol, but the cargo appears to be well stowed and in good condition. The boat returns to the *Dei Gratia* where, after a quarter-deck conference, it is decided that Mr. Deveau and seamen Augustus Anderson and Charles Lund shall comprise a salvage crew to sail the *Mary Celeste* to Gibraltar, 600 miles to the eastward.

Again aboard the derelict, Deveau and his two-man crew, tackle the work of putting her in order. After three hours at the pumps she is free of water and remains so with only 25 strokes night and morning. The vessel below the waterline is in good condition, but two days more are spent in repairing the running rigging and getting sail on her, showing how badly she is cut up aloft.

On December 13 the *Mary Celeste* arrives in port. She is immediately taken possession of by the British authorities. Captain Morehouse files a claim for salvage. Her case is brought before the Vice-Admiralty Court of Sir James Cochrane. Mr. Deveau is the principal witness before the Court. He handles himself admirably, giving a clear description of all details of which he has first knowledge. It is from this testimony that the bulk of the facts are available.* Mr. Deveau's statements are well supported by those of Second Mate Wright and Seaman Lund and Anderson. The Surveyor of Shipping, John Austin, makes a searching examination of the brigantine and among other points in his report, he states positively that the vessel had not been on her beam-ends, nor had she been boarded by a heavy sea. Asked as to the source of the water found below, he has no suggestion to offer.

Every effort of the Queen's Prosecuting officer

*The Court's proceedings may be found in the unabridged edition of that excellent book, "The Mary Celeste. The Odyssey of an Abandoned Ship," by Charles Edey Fay.

to make a case of violence proves futile—there is no
evidence to support it. The discovery of an old
sword in the captain's cabin is seized upon, but
the stains, upon examination, are not the result of
blood. After the Court's exhaustive investigation
no reason is found for the vessel's abandonment
and singular condition—no clue is developed as to
the cause of the damage. Consul Horatio Sprague
reports to the U.S. State Department that he has
no explanation.

Although the Honourable Mr. Sprague in
close touch with the conditions found aboard the
ship, had no theory to offer, there was no dearth
of imaginative minds to bring forth solutions
aplenty. They weirdly ranged through murder,
mutiny, piracy, a giant octopus, appearing and
disappearing islands. The theory most frequently
advanced and given considerable credence, dwells
on the dangers of the alcohol cargo. It puts forward the belief that vapours arising visibly from
the forward hatch led the crew to become alarmed
by the delusion of fire. This would indeed have
been alarming in view of the inflammable nature
of the cargo. This possibility has received a due
amount of attention.

The cargo when eventually delivered in Genoa
was checked out with a loss of nine out of 1,700
barrels of alcohol (proof 93.35, specific gravity
0.815). This shortage was not considered excessive
and the consignment was accepted. It would
appear that those nine barrels were errors in check-

ing. How much seepage, or actual flow into the hold is, of course, not known. If we grant that several barrels escaped through leakage it is believed that the point can still be made that alcohol was not the cause of the disaster.

Any definite leakage would have found its way into the bilges where it would have mingled with the bilge water. As it was the custom in wooden ships to sound the wells and pump ship each morning, there would have been a diminution of the alcoholic content at each pumping. It is conceded that there might well have been some vapours from this source. It is however, worthy of notice that no one of the investigators was sufficiently impressed to mention any odour of alcohol.

To support the idea of dangerous seepage the temperature difference between New York and the Azores has been used, and exaggerated. The average difference is not large. The mean temperature of the water in New York Harbour around the first of November is about 56° F.; that of the Gulf Stream where and when the *Celeste* crossed, ranges from 65° to 80° and off Santa Maria Island 66° F. The mean temperature of the air in the approaches to New York Harbour in November is close to 50° F. and off Santa Maria 65°-66° F. It will be seen that the mean differential is near 15° F. It is not believed that this change in temperature would have caused a dangerous condition or helped materially to increase the seepage.

A high authority on alcohol has been consulted in this connection and the opinion is that under the circumstances, no visible vapours would have been created. Unless proved otherwise this would discredit the idea that vapour "smoke" rising from the hatch produced a scare. However, an explosive mixture might have existed below, but the important point is that if fumes had, however unlikely, so united with the air in the hold as to form that nicely balanced explosive combination, which a spark from the friction of metal bands could ignite, there is little doubt that the result would have been so destructive as to leave no question of what happened to the *Mary Celeste*. Furthermore, it would have been a singular situation if fire had not ensued.

Instead, we have Mr. Austin's careful examination (5 hours) revealing that there was no evidence of an explosion; nor was any such evidence shown after the Marshall of the Court, Mr. Vecchio, had removed the main hatch, discharged 50 barrels, and made an inspection of the cargo, nor, again, in Genoa when all the consignment was turned over to the consignee. Also, the testimony of Mr. Deveau, who upon first going aboard saw no trace of smoke or fire, should be included. We are led to the firm conclusion that alcohol was not the cause of the crew's hasty departure.

There was an explanation of this mystery, current in the past, that received the advocacy of some seamen. It carried a degree of plausibility until closely analysed. The theory was that the brigantine had, on the morning of November 25, become becalmed and carried helpless by strong currents towards the Dollabarat Rocks that lie about 20 miles to the northeastward from Santa Maria. That nearing the breakers the crew took to the boat and were eventually lost in attempting to make a landing, or were swamped, while the vessel was carried safely by the danger.

This supposition is based on the weather record stating that calms and light airs prevailed among the Islands on that morning. It appears that there were but two weather stations in the Azores in 1872; one at Punta del Gada some 50 miles to the northward and at Terceira about 137 miles to the northwestward from the *Mary Celeste*'s position. We should, of course, accept the report as accurate for the conditions at the stations. It does not, however, inform us as to the winds near Santa Maria. There are instances where, at Cape Cod Lighthouse, there is a wind of 40 miles an hour and 20 miles to the westward there are light airs.

That morning (November 25) the brigantine was carrying the same reduced canvas as of the night before. Who ever heard of a skipper who failed to set sail immediately when the weather moderated! Surely not able Captain Briggs, nor Mr. Richardson when the "Old Man" was below. The fact is, no additional sail was set aboard the *Mary Celeste* before "something happened." We are forced to the opinion that the vessel was not in a calm nor did she drift near the Dollabarats.

Another suggestion has been made by reasoning people that Captain Briggs unrove and used the peak halyards as a tow-rope for the yawl in order to maintain contact with the vessel. The question of the peak halyards is perplexing, the testimony is at variance. Mr. Deveau stated that the halyards were "broke"; what became of the end is not definitely known.

Some one of the crew of the *Dei Gratia* is quoted as saying the peak halyards were "gone". In sailors' language that means parted, as well as lost. If a man at a wheel sees the jib sheet part, he would shout down the companion-way to the skipper, "The jib sheet's gone". In Admiral Smyth's "Sailors Word Book" of 1867, (contemporary with the period of this problem), we find, "GONE, Carried away. 'The hawser or cable is gone'; parted, broken."

Surveyor Austin in his report stated that the halyards he inspected were old, had been used for some time, and had not been spliced. It is not conceivable that Mr. Deveau would have been mistaken in saying that these halyards were parted when he went aboard, but there is some doubt whether they had been unrove. However, it is beyond belief that this observant mate looking for clues, would not have made much of such significant evidence.

Captain Briggs was surely in great haste to get clear of the ship. He was more intent on getting away than in holding fast to her. He didn't even lash the wheel (helm) alee—the work of a moment, an instinctive act of a good seaman. This would have aided in holding her to the wind. Otherwise if any doubt existed among them, it would seem, that Mr. Richardson would have remained aboard until he was certain that she was going down. Captain Briggs had an extreme incentive to be sure, wife, child and heavy investment in the vessel. His impulse was to take, what he thought was, the last desperate chance of saving their lives—doubtless in their minds they were sure the brigantine was about to founder.

To take the time to unreeve the peak halyards is not consonant with the other evidences of hurry. It may be well to explain that these halyards raise and support the end of the main gaff. The "standing part" is made fast to the end of the gaff; it is then led to a sheave in a trible block at the masthead, back to a single block some feet from the end of the gaff, again to the second sheave of the mast-head block, back to another single block some feet farther in from the first single block, then for the last time to the third sheave of the trible block and down at least 40 feet to the deck. It is estimated that this line would be close to 240 feet long. To haul that much fairly heavy rope through five sheaves and keep it from fouling, would be a time-consuming task, even for good seamen, under the peculiar conditions prevailing. It is not reasonable that the captain would do this.

Furthermore, it is believed that he and the mate

were too good sailors to attempt to ride to a tow-rope fast to a vessel with enough sail set to drag their small boat under the considerable sea that was running. One must not forget in this connection that when the wind got into that lower topsail the headway would have been considerable; the ship was not hove-to—her wheel (helm) was *not* alee.

Should the halyard have been merely parted and the end recovered, Mr. Deveau would have put in a "long splice" and restored it to service. This type of splice, when well done, is not easily detected. Whether Mr. Austin was seaman enough to note such a repair job is, of course not known. To put forward the premise that the halyards were only parted would admittedly be straining at apparently reliable testimony, yet it draws heavily on one's credulity that Mr. Deveau should have found an old set of peak halyards, rove them off and not seen and mentioned the outstanding import of the absence of those halyards from the gaff.

Mr. John Austin made a point in his report that a hawser, in the fore hold, under the hatch, was dry and he did not believe it had been wet. This may or may not be taken as an attempt to discredit Mr. Deveau's statement that there was, when he went aboard, "a great quantity of water" in the 'tween decks. It is assumed that the water reported was retained there by the height of the coamings of the 'tween deck hatch. As the hawser was stated to have been coiled directly under the fore hatch of the spar or upper deck, then it was probably on the lower hatch raised a little above the water that Mr. Deveau so carefully observed. Had the hawser been wet on November 25 it had four weeks in which to dry before Mr. Austin inspected it on December 23—much of the time with an open hatch just above it. There is no evidence for or against the possibility that the salvage crew had not taken the coil from some drier location and placed it beneath the fore hatch. They must have searched the lockers there for they found a spare try-sail which they brought up and used as a fore-sail.

The evidence indicates that the causing action of this disaster was not within the ship. There were no signs of violence, no suggestion of mutiny or drunkenness, barratry was obviously eliminated from any speculation, and the cargo only a remote possibility. The next step should be to seek an explanation from some outside destructive source. The blown away sails are glaring testimony pointing to excessive wind.

To the advocates of the explosion of vapour theory the questions are asked: "Why the blown out sails? Why the water below?" These proponents hasten to suggest that a squall struck the vessel subsequent to the crew's departure. This would mean that the yawl was launched from the brigantine with five sails set and she, not hove-to-her wheel (helm) as already stated, was not lashed alee and her yards were nearly square. This

c

would have presented quite a remarkable trick of seamanship. To get the loaded yawl safely away from the side of the ship *after* the sails were blown away was a skillful and dangerous task, but to do so with five sails set would have vastly increased the difficulties—to put it mildly. A seaman thinking about this would become doubtful that Captain Briggs left the vessel *before* the sails were lost. Hence, we are led to conclude that he departed *after* they were blown away and that their loss was directly connected with the abandonment.

Let us now begin a careful analysis of the clues to be found in the testimony given before the Court at Gibraltar and see where they lead:

The manner in which the crew left the vessel is easily cleared up. It is undeniable that there was only one boat aboard the *Celeste* and that boat was gone when the derelict was discovered. So, it is obvious that the crew abandoned her under some delusion of impending disaster. In the quest of this phantom we are immediately confronted by the mentioned fact of sails blown away, which conclusively suggests wind, and nothing else. We become puzzled by the testimony that three small hatches were off when first boarded and they were lying on the deck. It is quite evident that they were either lifted off by the crew or were blown up. Why the crew should have run around lifting hatches is not easy to understand; it is more logical, with the circumstances shown, to believe that they were blown off by some internal pressure. Furthermore, it is perplexing to account for the quantities of water reported in the 'tween decks, the galley and cabin. Yet singularly, the vessel was later found to be only leaking a small normal amount. Not coming through the bottom, the water must have come in the hatches, companionways and skylight (which was over the cabin, and up). Subsequently competent examiners testified that the vessel had not been boarded by a heavy sea nor had she been on her beam-ends. This being accepted as true, the water must have come from above and after the hatches and skylight had been thrown open.

There is no explanation that meets all these conditions of damage but a waterspout, whose characteristics are: a vicious wind: a radical difference in barometric pressure between, that within the spout and that outside, and an accompanying deluge of water. The results aboard the *Celeste* point definitely to such an encounter, in which the sails go, the hatches fly off, the water swirls below.

If you have been persuaded to take further interest in the waterspout theory, let us study this curious whirlwind for a few moments. On the land it is called a twister or tornado. At sea they are twisting columns of whirling wind and water, occurring almost anywhere, at any time, although more frequently met in the tropics. Within the spout the barometric pressure is *extra-ordinarily low*. They are seen in a great variety of forms, some from low clouds are short and thick, others high and thin, some move rapidly, others remain almost stationary. Their intensity varies from harmless to destructive; they twist and turn, slanting or erect.

While it is rare that a vessel is struck by a spout, it is by no means unique. Let me give an instance of what can happen and what was done to the bark *Ceylon*: On April 10, 1885, while in lat. 31° N., lg. 71° W., she was stripped of her canvas, the main and mizzenmasts were carried away, the mate was killed and the master injured. The report of this accident is taken from an article on waterspouts by the late Willis E. Hurd (formerly of the U. S. Weather Bureau) which appeared on the backs of many issues of the pilot charts of the Hydrographic Office of the Navy.

If a recent instance is preferred we have one in 1956: An AP despatch dated January 15 gives us the information that a tug with eight barges, 7 miles off the coast of Japan, was engulfed in a waterspout of great size. As a result of this encounter four men were killed or drowned, three barges were sunk and the rest that remained afloat, were damaged. The survivors were "dazed" but reported that the spout carried water and spume to a great height.

In browsing through the pages of very old issues of the Nautical Magazine of Glasgow this interesting, though not conclusive, item was found. Captain Steele of the ship *Mersey*, Liverpool for Oporto, Portugal, in 1842, when 36 miles off the coast, observed a waterspout passing three ship's lengths from his vessel. There was a small schooner 1½ miles ahead on the same course under a great press of sail. The weather was thick with thunder and lighting as the spout passed ahead in the direction of the schooner. When it cleared 15 minutes later, the schooner was not to be seen either from the deck or from aloft.

There is the case of the steamer *British Marquis* which shows the difficulty of avoiding a spout; and that they occur in high latitudes and in winter: In December 1920 while steaming up the English Channel, 20 waterspouts were sighted within two hours; she succeeded in avoiding those near at hand, until suddenly one formed directly ahead, sweeping across the decks with a screaming wind, which could readily have damaged a sailing craft.

Another interesting instance occurred in mid-Atlantic on March 30, 1923 at 2:23 a.m., when the White Star liner *Pittsburg* was struck head on by a waterspout damaging the bridge and chart room and flooding the officers' quarters.

In 1945 an interesting encounter took place in Chesapeake Bay, off Reedsville, Virginia, in which a sloop was thrown on her beam-ends with mast in the water. Mr. William H. Daniels, her owner, and skipper, writing in *Motor Boating* of November that year, stated that his wife and two daughters were below. Miss Mildred gave the apt description of their sensations as being in a "corn popper". Mr. Daniels added that he experienced *a mental blank as though he were in a vacuum*—very significant points of interest, giving an indication of the power within the spout. Many more instances could be enumerated were it necessary, but the point has been made that ships have been damaged by waterspouts.

The weather service record of the Azores Islands reveals that a depression was passing to the northward of the *Mary Celeste* and she, on November 24, was in the westerly winds of the southern semi-circle of this disturbance. In Mr. Hurd's pilot chart article on "Waterspouts" we learn that in the north temperate zone they tend to develop in the southeast and southwest quadrants of east-travelling depressions hence we see that the brigantine was in a favourable position for the occurrence of such a phenomenon. However, the probability is that no one aboard had even been close enough to a waterspout to comprehend its dangerous character.

Now being equipped with the main facts and essential phases of the known conditions let us endeavour to build a hypothetical case for the waterspout theory:

It is the morning of November 25 (civil date) Captain Briggs is tired after his broken night, but he is relieved as there are no shoals or islands ahead between him and the coast of Spain. He eats his breakfast and turns in. The mate is busy about the decks as mates always are, directing the routine duties of the watch. It is somewhere about 9:30

a.m. The cook, with his pots and pans all washed up, is relaxing before he starts the dinner. All is reasonably quiet and commonplace at that morning hour, and while the wind may have eased somewhat the vessel is still running off her 8 knots with wind still a little in the starboard quarter, sails trimmed for the starboard tack.

Suddenly, a shout of alarm sweeps through the brigantine. Aghast, they look off to windward to see a whirling, roaring waterspout close aboard. It is a terrifying sight, twisting in its erratic course, it swiftly turns and charges across the ship without a chance to avoid it. The vessel is engulfed in a screaming blast of wind and deluge of swirling water. The frightened crew hang fast to the nearest substantial object. The noise is terrifying; the vessel pulsates under a strange power. The barometer drops in an extraordinary manner, but no one cares or thinks to read it. The fore and lazarette hatches pop off (probably the galley scuttle), up goes the cabin skylight; it is all very weird. Wind driven water pours below, sails rip from the bolt ropes and running rigging, parting everywhere, is whipped in wild and noisy confusion. The water driving in under the skylight drenches the clock, soaks the captain's bed (from which he sprang at the first alarm) and leaves the whole cabin in a sodden condition.

In only a few moments the blast is over leaving in its wake a mentally disorganized crew. They seem numbed by a "vacuum-like" condition that has just passed. Captain Briggs, like the others, is shaken by the eerie calamity. His first fear is underwater damage and instinctively calls for sounding of the pump well. All hands are shocked by the shout:

"There's six feet in her." Six feet in 3 minutes!

"She's going down," some one cries. The fright is contagious—you can almost feel her going. Captain Briggs too feels it. . . .

"Clear away the boat." They rush eagerly to cut lashings, remove the ship's rail, the painter is led forward and the yawl is launched over the side into a rough sea. None stops for clothes, water or provisions; only the master thinks of anything; he grabs the ship's papers. Mrs. Briggs with baby are helped into the surging boat; the captain jumps as she luckily clears the side without swamping. They haul off, holding the small craft head to the sea as best they can. Suddenly Captain Briggs is shocked at the sight of the ship's freeboard. It is suspiciously high; he shouts to Mr. Richardson:

"Something's wrong. She's not sinking. Pull for the ship."

The oars are feeble in a wind and sea—the headway is slow. The head sails that are left set, begin to fill, her bow falls off. The wind gets into the hanging lower topsail, she gathers way and rushes off to the leeward. What a sight of despair for an able master to look upon! The tragedy is prolonged, for the vessel begins to come-to and loses way. Frantically they pull. Alas, the wind

again bears her off and once again she races away. At length exhausted they are left castaways in a small boat on a rough sea, without protection of adequate clothing or provisions.

Their ordeal of death was, no doubt, relatively short for a few hours later the wind blew a gale from the northwest creating a cross sea—too much for a small over-loaded boat. It was their friends and relatives in New England and the Friesian Islands who were to suffer years of uncertain grief.

One would be sanguine indeed, if he thought this sequence of events would bring conviction to this theory without a further attempt to clear up point by point the more obscure phases of the affair.

No doubt the first question would be: Why was the mistake made in the amount of water in the vessel?

The excessively low barometric pressure in the spout, being similar to that in a tornado ashore (where the explosive effect blows building walls *outward*) set up a sharp difference in pressure between the outside and inside of the hull, that in my belief, blew off the hatches and at the same time pushed bilge water up the pump well. For the pressure would have been on the bilge water as well as on all other surfaces within the hull. The lower box of the pump having a valve that would have allowed this upward flow, but prevented, at least for a time, its return to the hold when the pressure was released. When Captain Briggs heard that there was six in her (an amount guessed at) there was probably less than a foot actually in the hold, for she was leaking very little. Some of this water no doubt got through the hatches. There was a definite hint of this by Mr. Deveau who knew more about the *Celeste* than any man alive. He, when asked by the Court what, in his opinion, caused the abandonment, replied, "My idea is that the crew got alarmed and by the sounding rod being found alongside the pump, that *they had sounded the well and found a quantity of water in the pumps, at the moment, and thinking she would go down, abandoned her."*

Some people will want to know why the head sails should have remained intact when two square sails close by were blown away?

There could be at least two explanations of this situation. The damage by twisters ashore is freakish and a waterspout is a whirlwind on the sea. They often cut a narrow, sharply defined path leaving a tree or a building while demolishing others a few feet away. Another possible explanation is offered: The wind may have struck the plane of the jibs at a small angle, while the square sails at a broad angle with the jibs, caught the full impact. It is believed that the spout so approached that its whirling wind struck the after side of the square sails, which would be more or less in the plane of the jibs. The reason for this deduction is that a square sail "taken aback" is supported by the mast and rigging and is less liable to be split to pieces than from a wind from aft. But more conclusive was the condition of the lower top-sail;—the head of this sail having been ripped from the yard and held only by the heavy earrings at the ends of the yard. The sail was made fast at about 18 inch intervals to an iron rod (jackstay) set on and parallel to the top of the yard. Stout pieces of small tarred stuff called robands are used to secure the sail.

With the wind on the foreward side—sail aback—
the pressure on the sail on the forward side of the
yard would create a pronounced frictional support
which would relieve the robands of much of the
stress. While with the wind aft, the sail would be
lifted and the robands would necessarily take the
full stress. In this case they gave way.

There has always been a lively curiosity expressed concerning the easterly course made by
the *Mary Celeste* as she covered close to 370 miles
wholly unattended.

A fairly clear picture of her wandering may be
brought out by a close study of the known facts
using logical deductions therefrom. Competent
seamen agree in general that the bow of a sailing
vessel with little or no way on her, under two head
sails with sheets fast, and no after sail set,
would be borne off from the wind. In close quarters
a jib is used for that very purpose. The wind
during the period from November 25 to December 4 must have been predominantly from the
westward, otherwise the vessel could not have
accomplished that considerable distance. We know
at least that on the night of November 25 it blew
a gale from the north-west and Deveau stated
that for three days prior to December 4 the *Dei
Gratia* had experienced strong north-west winds.
On that day it blew heavily but had moderated to
a light northerly by afternoon. The westerly winds
must have been persistently strong for had they
become light, the pressure on the head sails would

have balanced the vessel's tendency to come-to at about five or six points from the wind. In this position she would have made little or no progress eastward (easting). This is the position that she assumed when found in the light northerly.

When the ship was borne off from the wind and it came well abaft the beam, the square lower topsail would have filled and given her substantial eastward headway. Then after running for a brief time her natural tendency to come-to would assert itself, and coming-to she would run off part of her headway. Then again the pressure on the head sails would bear her off and the sequence would be established. With westerly winds she would be making "easting" on a course, consisting of many curves.

It is a reasonable probability that she luffed and bore away on the port tack. In this way on each luff she would "eat" a little to the north, accounting for her "made good" (net) course of ENE which called for considerable "northing." Then again, on this tack, the port, *her head sails would have been aback*—to windward—very effective in bearing her head off. It will be remembered her sheets were trimmed for the starboard tack when found, as they were on the morning of November 25. The port (weather) lower topsail brace was not carried away and would have steadied the yard when the wind got into the sail. Had the brig been on the starboard tack (to westerly winds) during her fugitive sailing, she would have made a component of "southing" instead of "north-ing". This tends to support the port tack idea.

Many people have been puzzled by the fact that the *Mary Celeste* was heading westward when first sighted by the *Dei Gratia*.

There are some clues that will help to recon-struct her movements. With the two head sails set, and no after sail, one is quite safe in making the direct statement that she could not have tacked herself and doubtful if it could have been done with the crew aboard. Hence with tacking elimi-nated she must have gone around before the wind —manoeuvre known as "wearing ship". When she was borne away from the wind, by the pressure on the head sails, it only required some extra impetus, when going nearly before the wind, to cast her to the other tack. This impetus could have come from a sea heavier than others or at a different angle, rushing under the counter thrusting the stern to port (bow to starboard), and bringing the wind on the starboard quarter. (The possibility of a sea kicking the rudder over at the critical moment should not be entirely eliminated.) With the wind on the starboard quarter she would begin to luff and bear away as she had done on the port tack for many days. This thrust of a sea under the counter when running, was a very real condition in sailing vessels and required an expert helmsman to pre-vent a ship from broaching-to. It is believed that this explains a more likely manoeuvre than that she was brought around to the starboard tack by wind shifts.

On December 4 the strong westerly wind veering northerly became light. The *Mary Celeste* then on the starboard tack assumed a position heading westward with head sails' pressure balancing the vessel's tendency to come-to. With the light wind prevailing she kept her heading (within a small range of variation) around 70° (a little forward of the beam)—and that is the way she was found.

Again, there is the oft repeated question— "Why should a crew leave a vessel, taking to a small boat in a rough sea?"

In reply it may be said that seamen who harbour few fears have a distinct dread of going down with a ship. They stay until they feel sure she is sinking and the record of premature abandonments shows that they have been mistaken many times. To get clear of a sinking ship is with them a strong and understandable impulse. In an admirable book called "Lower Class," George Youell, a former Lowestoft fisherman, tells of his experience in a North Sea trawler during an historic gale. She was hove-to under three scraps of canvas in a furious wind and high running sea: "All of the men stayed on deck," wrote Mr. Youell, "though they might well have been below. Sailors always appear to have a preference for being drowned on deck or being washed off it, rather than drowning peacefully in their bunks."

A ship, in law, is a personality, she is compe-

tent to contract, is individually liable for her obli-
gations, she may sue in her owner's name and be
sued in her own. She may be placed under arrest.
Surely *Mary Celeste* acted a personality. Though
an innocent participator, she was deeply involved
in this tragedy. At the first opportunity she became a fugitive, rushing from the vicinity, then as
though she had the instincts of a criminal she
turned about as if to return to the scene of the
crime. She was, however, intercepted, taken possession of and sailed into Gibraltar where she was
put under arrest. There, the subject of the court
action, she proved a stubborn witness, as has been
seen, revealing nothing for the enlightenment of
the court or the baffled world at large. The personality of this trim brig *Mary Celeste* should be
honoured as a little lady who locked up a secret
—until, we hope, the waterspout becomes the key.

PART II

Sea Lore

These four turbulent
episodes have been selected
to help preserve the image of the
sailor of sail as a lusty battler against
the ferocious assaults of wind and weather. His
dominant ambition was not for gain, but to triumph
over the sea

D

On a Lee Shore

THE WILD drama of a square-rigged vessel battling off a lee shore is now a part of the romantic and often tragic past. The square rig, so efficient on the long thousand-mile reaches of favourable winds, was almost helpless when attempting to work to windward in gales and heavy seas. The odds were against a ship caught with land close to leeward; only a favourable trend of the coast, a shift of wind, or a benevolent current, offered an escape. The hard beset master, left with no hope but his anchors, had reached an extremity of peril, where if they failed to hold, he was left with the last resort of cutting away the masts. It was the lee shore that has accounted for a long dismal record of doomed vessels, from whose decks their crews were cast into roaring breakers, as their ships were pounded into wreckage on brutal coasts.

It is doubtful that in the history of the Navy, there has been a more remarkable escape from destruction on a lee shore than that of U.S.S. *Relief* in 1839. This ship was a unit of the U.S.

Exploring Expedition which was headed by Captain Charles Wilkes U.S.N. By splendid seamanship and rare good fortune, this vessel with anchors down, was held off the rocks of Noir Island, Tierra del Fuego, by a close margin.

The details of this classic experience recently came to light in the journal of Ezra Green, yeoman of that vessel. This admirable hour by hour record, set down by a practiced seaman, was discovered in the attic of the old Green home in Massachusetts, by a grandson, Colonel Jonathan H. Harwood. It is now preserved in the museum of the U.S. Navy Academy at Annapolis.

Ezra Green, a sailor of romance, left a cultured home in the environs of Boston to roam the seas, during which he served three or four hitches in the Navy. When the Wilkes Expedition was fitting out, under the auspices of the Hydrographic Office, men were enlisted for the duration of the cruise in order that the commanding officer might not be hampered by expiring enlistments. Green joined up, and though primarily a seaman, evidently became a yeoman through his gift in writing a splendid account of passing events—a talent useful in pursuing the object of the expedition. His story of the experience of the *Relief* at Noir Island checks well with that given by Captain Wilkes in his account of the U.S. Exploring Expedition. However, the latter quite naturally lacks the vividness of Green's description for Captain Wilkes was not there.

The five ships of the squadron had worked down the eastern coast of South America, gathering desired hydrographic and other information. The vessels did not always sail in company but separated as best served the purpose of the work. They were to double Cape Horn for an eventual rendezvous at Callao; one, the schooner *Sea Gull*, was lost with all hands on a rocky lee shore near the Cape where she was last seen. The *Relief*, under the skilful command of Lieutenant-Commander A. K. Long, got safely around the Horn, but was caught in a southwesterly gale uncomfortably close in on the iron-bound coast of Tierra del Fuego.

On the morning of March 18, 1839, with the gale making, the *Relief* was hove-to hoping the weather would change for the better. The land was under their lee, shut out by the thick weather. At 11 a.m. it was blowing a gale; the ship was lying under close-reefed main-topsail and fore-storm-staysail. They began to entertain doubts as to their ability to hold off the coast. This anxiety was confirmed when the ship was struck by a violent hail squall, which cleared the air somewhat, revealing Noir Island only about 12 miles to leeward. All hope of weathering that coast was then abandoned and Captain Long boldly decided to run for the open roadstead of that island. The main-topsail was taken in and the ship put off before the wind under several fore and aft sails. Recurring hail squalls were so dense as to shut out all sight of the land. In fact they narrowly missed the off-lying

Tower Rocks that suddenly appeared close aboard to starboard over which the surf broke furiously, as it was also off to port, on the south-western point of Noir Island. Captain Long climbed aloft and from a position on the fore-yard conned the vessel with his trumpet, avoiding sunken rocks with seamanly judgment. After passing Tower Rocks for some distance, they began to haul up for an anchorage. The sea eased somewhat as they got a little lee from the island.

As the purpose of the expedition was to gather information and descriptions, Yeoman Green, true to laid-down routine, began to describe the aspect of the land, but quickly broke off saying quaintly, "our minds, however, were too much occupied by the contemplation of the awful sea spread out to our view, for us to be close observers of landmarks."

At about 6 p.m. they got soundings which quickly shoaled to 17 fathoms. They then luffed sharply, took in all sails and let go both bower anchors, veering chain to the bitter ends—150 fathoms. To cut windage aloft the t'gallant-masts were struck (sent down) and yards braced to the wind. As a precaution at 7:30 p.m., the port sheet anchor (sheet anchors were the heaviest) was dropped underfoot with chain slack. During that night, March 18-19, there was no abatement in the gale, but their position was made more hazardous by the backing of the wind to the eastward of south (magnetic). They were then exposed to the

U.S.S. *Relief*

full sweep of the open ocean to the south. At this point Green praises the quality of their ground tackle but, "had it been that of a line-of-battleship it could not long have withstood this."

In the north-eastern part of Noir Road there is a reef making out with a higher rock at its outer extremity. With the wind as it was then blowing, this rock was immediately astern of the heavily riding ship with little room to spare. The seas breaking ferociously so close astern gave them a clear picture of their impending fate. They could hold no hope that there would be any survivors if the ship once struck the reef. Any who might have survived drowning would have been beaten to death against the rocks or if the shore were reached, died of exposure. It was a situation almost beyond hope.

At 6 p.m., of the 19th there was a heavy shock on the port bower cable and the ship began to drag, taking the slack of the port sheet anchor until it shared the terrific stress. Captain Long then ordered the starboard sheet anchor let go. All the ship's four heavy anchors were then out and there was little more to be done, of which Green writes, "We resigned ourselves to whatever fate our God might have in store for us."

About midnight March 19-20, a heavy rain seemed to abate the violence of the gale for a few hours but only to gather further fury. At daylight of the 20th, they were dismayed to find that the ship had dragged considerably during the night, bringing the anchors into less favourable holding ground. The port sheet anchor cable was found slack and upon heaving it in, discovered that it had parted at the 45-fathom shackle. The yeoman bemoans this loss, it being, "our very best cable; its loss would be felt at any time, now the loss was more severe from its being irreparable." Becoming suspicious as to the condition of the port bower, it was hove in and they found the anchor broken at the stock. This accounted for the shock of the evening before. A deeper gloom was thrown over the ship's company as they had lost two of their four heavy anchors and the gale continued in all its violence.

It is evident that owing to the remote and savage region they were in, Captain Long, even at this critical juncture, never entertained the thought of cutting away the masts. No mention of such an act appears in the records. They would have been left without power to escape and beyond rescue. Those were no waters in which to venture under a jury rig and Captain Wilkes would have had no knowledge of their whereabouts. So they held on as best they could, placing any remaining faith in their anchors. No doubt it was such dramatic situations as this that created the anchor as the "emblem of hope". There aboard the *Relief* they even got out a stream anchor backed by a kedge, but such light gear was futile where the great sheet anchor had failed. It, no doubt, was good for the mind to be busy at anything under the circumstances. The usual behaviour of a gale from this quarter was to veer to the westward, which would again have given them a partial lee, but their trust in this change was dashed as, towards night, (20th) the gale backed to the SSE with increased intensity. They then became convinced that their end was imminent. It proved a night of horror; they prayed for daylight in which to make their last battle in the surf, as the squalls came in greater frequency and added fury. Green writes that, "the noise made by the chain cables as they dragged on the rocky bottom was the most awful noise I ever heard and the Lord grant I may never hear it again." The ship became an immense sounding board. Again he said, "The starboard bower was our mainstay; it held on most nobly."

During the evening the men were sent below for food and drink, only to be immediately returned to their stations as the ship was dragging nearer to the rocks astern. At 11:30 p.m., March 20, they dragged across the tail of the reef just clearing the mentioned rock at its outer end. This position brought the vessel into the breaking seas, one of which broke aboard in a deluge, filling the decks, washing the men about and pouring down the hatches. The two anchors out caught on the edge of the reef and with the ship in these breakers, the cables parted with a great shock; another sea was shipped, again filling the decks. Then, strangely, after this disaster, the wind eased. The ship continued to drag with her anchorless chains trailing

along the bottom. It was a miracle. They slipped
the cables when Astronomers Point bore WSW,
wore ship under the fore-trysail and storm-stay-
sails; reefed courses and main-trysail soon followed.
"The wind now through the goodness of God moderated and shifted to SSW." More sail was set;
the stars came out and after midnight the storm
abated. "There were not," commented Green, "a
few hearts that did not silently and sincerely thank
God. . . .". On March 21, "All hands were called to
'splice the main brace' and bid a hearty farewell to
Noir Island."

When the *Relief* arrived anchorless off the
port of Valparaiso at sunset of April 13, she could
not enter. Lying off and on, a boat was sent in and
as Captain Wilkes states in his account: Captain
Locke of *Her Britannic Majesty's Ship Fly,* "in a
most prompt and handsome manner," sent an
anchor out to the *Relief.* She was then able to
enter port for rest and refreshment.

EPILOGUE[1]

Ezra Green came from old stock and carried
the name of a distinguished uncle, who served as
John Paul Jones's surgeon in the famous *Ranger.*[2]
Off the entrance of Belfast Lough in 1778 when
the U.S.S. *Ranger* and the H.B.M.S. *Drake* fought
for an hour, this uncle had plenty of grisly work
to do.[3] So through this background we have a hint
as to the nephew's inspiration for the sea.

After a four years' cruise, with the Wilkes expedition and with many adventures, Ezra Green was discharged at New York in August 1842. He immediately proceeded to his home in Malden, Massachusetts, walking in on his surprised family, who had give him up for lost. The sailor, then 42 years of age, announced that he was giving up the sea.

In a very few days he decided to go on a hunting trip up in Vermont and accordingly took a stage for those parts. While so travelling he became strongly attracted to a young and lovely passenger who so charmed him that when she left the stage at Landgrove, he forthwith abandoned his hunting plans and followed. Landing, a stranger, in this manner at the centre of a rural New England village, called for a liberal measure of tact to gain the information he desired. It soon became evident that Ezra Green had not sailed the seas all those years without acquiring other knowledge than reefing topsails, for he not only learned the girl's name from those taciturn Vermonters, but the location of her home—a farm outside the village.

It so happened that he was walking past this farm the next day just before noon; he became thirsty, and singularly enough, he arrived at the pump in the yard coincident with the farmer's habit of washing his hands for dinner. With appropriate comment on the excellence of the water, compared with what he had drunk all over the world, he caught he farmer's interest, who hospitably invited him to dinner. One has to respect the old sailor's technique, for there in the dining room was the farmer's daughter. Even in this unaccustomed situation Green was a man of action, for in two or three weeks, Elmina Minerva Richardson, his 20-year-old bride, was carried back to Malden, giving his family two pleasant surprises in a month.

Ezra Green died on the twentieth anniversary of his happy marriage. Mrs. Green survived him by 43 years. She was a remarkable woman, left with limited means and eight children, she contrived to support and educate them. Her eldest son, Bernard R. Green, became a distinguished engineer. He was called to Washington by Colonel Thomas Lincoln Casey, U.S. Corps of Engineers, then in charge of Federal construction in the national capital. The Washington Monument was up one-third of its height and leaning. Engineer Green devised a new foundation, righted the shaft and largely superintended its completion; he was later the constructing engineer of the Library of Congress.

It has been my good fortune and pleasure to have known three generations of this accomplished family, whose crest should be an anchor in tribute to that faithful starboard bower that held the *Relief* so long from the breakers of Noir Island.

1. From information set down by Colonel Jonathan H. Harwood of East Greenwich, R.I., and conversations with Dr. Julia M. Green, M.D., of Washington, D.C., a granddaughter.
2. Diary of Ezra Green (1746-1847).

3. The *Ranger* and the *Drake* had exchanged broadsides in an action that Jones described as "warm, close and obstinate," and which proved the latter ship's misfortune. Soon Dr. Green was a busy surgeon working among the many wounded of the *Drake's* people; the *Ranger* lost only eight in killed and wounded. Notable in his operations was the amputation of Thomas Huggan's leg shattered by a six-pound shot. He was the *Drake's* surgeon, a rare character, better known in the Royal Navy as Old Bacchus, obviously due to his convivial propensities.

Jones, after making repairs to his badly cut up prize, was determined to take her into a French port, despite alerted frigates of the enemy. Upon successfully arriving in Quiberon Bay, he received the first salute to the American flag by a foreign power. Captain Jones had won a minor, though brilliant victory, yet through political repercussions it became a strong influence in bringing France into war with England. There in France, Doctors Green and Bacchus, brought together in sanguinary violence, parted their ways and for a time disappeared from the record.

When the *Ranger* left for home (without Jones who went on to further glory) it is highly probable that Dr. Green returned in her to America. We later find him practising medicine in Dover, N.H., where he lived until he was 101 years of age.

Old Bacchus romantically reappears, with a peg leg, as the surgeon of *H.M.S. Bounty* in 1787. If you will turn to page 30 of Nordorf's and Hall's "Mutiny on the Bounty," you will find him there telling his shipmates how the surgeon of Paul Jones's *Ranger* amputated his leg with a crosscut saw, a well-stropped razor and a pint of rum.

The Sloop Granite

I N APRIL, 1851, during a memorable storm on
  the coast of Massachusetts, Minot's Ledge
Lighthouse was carried away and its keepers lost.
This aid to navigation was, and is, highly important
as it protects the mariner against the dangerous
ledge lying in the south-eastern approach to Boston
harbour. The problem of erecting a new and more
substantial tower was extremely difficult to solve.
The sea, almost always breaking on the rocks, leaves
them exposed only a few hours a month during
the low water of spring tides (twice a month) and
then the sea must be calm.

Owing to these adverse conditions it took
several years for the engineers to obtain a relief
plan of the ledge's form and to shape blocks of
granite to dovetail into the irregularities of the
rocky foundation. Among the equipment necessary
for this work was a small sailing vessel, built to
unusually heavy specifications. It was her job to
transfer the blocks of granite on the short haul
from the Quincy quarries to the ledge. Her oak

planking was of a thickness that would stand the shock of an occasional crash upon the rocks. Ap propriately, her name was *Granite*.

When a vessel slides down the launching ways the onlookers invariably speculate on what her future holds and what her end may be. But it is doubtful if any of those who saw the lowly *Granite* become water borne, imagined that this work horse of the ledges would rise to a unique naval career.

Soon after the *Granite* finished her rugged service in the turbulent surges of Minot's Ledge the Civil War began. Then, as in every conflict, the government began making use of almost anything that would float. It was hardly conceivable that the sloop *Granite* could be adapted to a warfare that even then was preponderately under steam power, but like many another queer craft she was caught in the dragnet. Her armament was a 32 pounder weighing 57,000 pounds, mounted on deck, and she assumed the dignified status of a naval gunboat. Early in the war she was in the Chesapeake area doing useful odd jobs and then further down at Hatteras Inlet, far from the quarries of Quincy.

The *Granite* was in the charge of two men who were well fitted to her rugged character, each with the rank of acting master's mate. They bore names which, through the fleet, were corrupted derisively into Bummer and Loafer. Bummer was in command and Loafer was the mate. There was said to have been little social intercourse between the officers of the *Granite* and those of the North Atlantic Blockading Squadron to which she belonged. The situation was, no doubt, something more than agreeable to Bummer and Loafer. Nevertheless what these men may have lacked in the gentle amenities was more than balanced by the prime seamanship with which the *Granite* was handled on all occasions.

At Hatteras Inlet early in 1862 she was in a strategic spot. Flag Officer L. M. Goldsborough was preparing to take control of the North Carolina Sounds by way of this inlet, thereby cutting the Confederacy's inland navigation and stopping annoying raids. The first objective of the federal forces was the forts on and opposite Roanoke Island, located in the southeast corner of Albemarle Sound. There were 25 heavy guns, three 100 pounders, on the island, eight at Fort Forest opposite to the west and 16 aboard the Confederate gunboats cooperating with the forts. General Ambrose Burnside had been ordered to work with the navy. On January 28 1862, there were 18 Federal gunboats concentrated in the southern part of Pamlico Sound about 40 miles from Roanoke Island and on February 5 the army had arrived in transports and was ready.

Croatan Sound, in which the battle was fought, lying between Roanoke Island and the mainland to the west, is of small extent and shoal. Hence this expedition was hampered by being restricted to vessels of the light draft of seven feet.

E

Some of the gunboats had less than a foot beneath their keels at times while manoeuvring in action.

At the north-western end of Roanoke Island it was only 2½ miles to the mainland lying westward and the sides of this passage were fortified— Pork Point and Weirs Point on the island and Fort Forrest at Redstone Point opposite. Furthermore, a line of obstructions, consisting of sunken vessels and piles, had been placed by the enemy in the passage between the forts. A fleet of eight Confederate gunboats was stationed behind the obstructions. On February 7 the federal expeditions began feeling out the enemy and by noon the action became general. At 1:30 p.m. the barracks at Pork Point were afire. At 3 p.m., the army began to land at Ashbys' Harbour and by midnight 10,000 troops were ashore. The next morning, February 8 1862, at 9 a.m. both the navy and the army attacked, the latter getting into the rear of the fortifications. At 1 p.m. nine vessels were detached to clear the obstructions and at four o'clock they broke through. In a short time Pork Point was taken. The enemy set Fort Forrest afire at Redstone Point and it blew up in the evening. The area was soon in Union hands.

In the initial plan a gunboat was to tow the *Granite* into action, in this way bringing her 32 pounder into use. However, one can understand how irksome, under the circumstances, this hindrance could be for the commander of the towing vessel and somehow after a short time those in the *Granite* found themselves left adrift. Bummer and Loafer, besides having those desirable qualities of clear thinking and cool acting, were not of a breed of seamen to drift in sight of a fine battle when there was a chance to be in it.

A favourable wind was blowing and they quickly made sail. Without waiting for specific orders they loaded their gun and sailed directly past Pork Point fort, firing rapidly. Having a beam or so-called soldier's wind, they came about, reloaded, repassed and passed again; even at times, it was said, inside other ships.

The solid oak hull of the *Granite*, built to stand against the shocks of Minot's Ledge, was good armour for gunfire, but no shot struck her that day. After the battle of Roanoke Island there was a marked reaction throughout the fleet. Bummer, gaining respect, even becoming a hero, was soon promoted from master's mate to master.

Sea history is largely based on logbooks and official reports, yet every officer with experience at sea knows that much human interest and some details of fact fail to be recorded in the logbook, especially if the officer holds an awkward pen. Hence it is that personal narrative, carefully weighed for reasonable accuracy, becomes an important source of history. The above account of Bummer's activities came to me in this manner from my uncle, a Coast Survey officer who was on duty in the North Carolina sounds shortly after the battle. There has never been an occasion when it was felt necessary to check that officer's relation of events, but curiosity led me to consult the Civil War records regarding the activities of the sloop-rigged *Granite* (not to be confused with *sloop of war* which was used to designate the larger three masted vessel).

It was found that Bummer was in reality Ephram Boomer and the record shows that he was indeed promoted from acting master's mate to acting master. The report of Lt. A. Murray, commanding the second column at the Battle of Roanoke Island states in part: "The sloop *Granite*, Master's Mate Ephram Boomer, cmdg., left out in the early part of the action, being entirely dependent on her sail, finally worked up to close quarters with the enemy and bearing his part gallantly throughout."

Boomer's own classic report to Flag Officer L. M. Goldsborough could be used as an example by those admirals who are advocates of brevity and it was truly in character:

U.S. Sloop Granite

Croatan Sound, Feb,11, 1862

Sir:

I most respectfully report that during the action of the 7th and 8th instant. I expended 26,

5-second and 4, 10-second shell and 16 solid shot, 46, 8-pound charges. Casualties none; injured none.

I am very respectfully your obedient servant,

> E. Boomer,
> Acting Master's Mate,
> Commanding U.S. Sloop Granite.
> Flag Officer L. M. Goldsborough.

The 46 charges for one gun indicate creditable activity. If the suggestion is not refuted by some later instance it may be that the little *Granite* has the distinction of being the last American naval vessel to engage in an organized battle under sail alone.

The Cold Call of Duty

TREMENDOUS is the word to describe the violence of the great storm of March, 1888. It savagely lashed all shipping off the Atlantic coast from Montauk, Long Island, to and below Cape Hatteras. Beyond this area of fury, gales extended northward to the Gulf of St. Lawrence and southward to the Florida Keys. Over 200 vessels were driven ashore, foundered or heavily damaged. There are a few left, after over 75 years, who remember its havoc, but for 50 years and more it was the measuring rod of all later storms off that coast. The furious wind drove the snow into drifts of incredible depths and completely paralysed the city of New York. Birds in great numbers on their spring flight northward were swept out to sea and lost.

Amid all the devastation on land and sea perhaps the New York (and New Jersey) Pilot Association suffered the most. Of the 19 schooners they had out on March 11 only three returned undamaged. Two foundered with all hands, nine were driven ashore, two were in collision, two on their beam ends and one limped in with steering gear damaged.

Those were the days when the pilots operated their schooners each as a private venture and all in sharp competition. Some sailed far to the south-eastward and southward to meet shipping from that direction, while others pressed eastward, even to meridian 62° W, some 550 miles from Sandy Hook, to pick up ships from Europe. Out there in the near and distant approaches to New York, the able little schooners took the weather as it came, winter and summer, but in 1888 it was something else again.

On Sunday, March 11, the day started mild and pleasant with spring in the air. About noon it became overcast with a gentle rain; the barometer showing no indication of a remarkable change. Nevertheless, about 3 p.m., some of the weather-wise pilots sensed something ominous and several headed for shelter at Sandy Hook. Other than their observation of the sky, air and sea they had no way of knowing that a tremendous storm was in the making. In fact a low trough extending from above the Great Lakes southward to the Gulf of Mexico, had been moving eastward, holding a north-south axis. As it approached the coast, warm damp air from over the Gulf Stream was feeding in from the southeast and the trough deepened rapidly. Its northern end, upon reaching New York on the night of the 11th, began to cushion against a high atmospheric area located east of New England. This high served as a barrier, delaying the eastward movement of the storm. The southern end, in the meantime, was unimpeded and began to swing offshore, pivoting on the nearly stationary northern end.

Snow began to fall lightly about midnight of the 11th. Four hours later the sleeping pilots in the schooners, anchored in the normally safe Horseshoe of Sandy Hook, were roused out by dragging anchors. Second anchors with long scopes failed to stop them in the worst northwest blizzard they had ever seen. This was the furious wind tearing down the western side of the trough.

Those vessels outside and more to the eastward reported that the central line of the trough passed over them with a short respite that lay between a warm southeast gale and the bitter cold nor'wester. The impact of the swift transition was terrific on both men and vessels. Due to the delayed movement of the northern end of the depression the storm was of extreme duration in the vicinity of New York. It continued to blow with hurricane force, snow and sleet, until around 4 p.m. of the 13th.

Among the schooners that rode out the great storm at sea was the *Charles H. Marshall*. She was 78 feet in length and at 28 years was getting old for such a beating. Her builder in 1860 must have been a faithful artisan, and the pilots good to her, for she proved herself a worthy vessel. Many years ago in the Hydrographic Office I stumbled on a report of her experience in 1888. It was a cryptic account of the vessel's splendid battle against winds gone wild. It shows the resourcefulness of the crew and their fine, though seemingly unconscious, sense of duty.

At 9 a.m., March 11, this vessel was 18 miles off Barnegat Light. The wind was freshening from the southeast and the crew turned in a reef in the foresail and one in the main. Soon the weather worsened and they were obliged to further shorten down. Becoming suspicious of conditions, they headed northward for shelter. By 4 p.m., they had three reefs in the mainsail, with jib furled. The warm air coming from over a warmer sea met cooler temperatures and caused a dense fog, which led those in the *Marshall* to abandon the attempt to make port. She was hove-to on the starboard tack, heading eastward, being then about 18 miles southeast of Sandy Hook Lightship.

At 3 a.m., on March 12, the low pressure trough was reaching the coast. The sky to the north-west became so threatening in appearance that a fourth reef was turned in the mainsail and the foresail was triple reefed—none too soon. At 3:30 a.m., the weather changed abruptly. The wind fell to a calm with the vessel labouring in a tremendous southeast sea which threatened to swamp her. In 20 minutes the wind came out of the northwest with a ferocious blast that knocked the schooner down on her beam ends. Usually this is a critical situation but here the *Marshall*'s fine design was manifested as she righted herself. The wind then pulling frigid air from behind the cold front caused the warm temperatures to tumble to zero in a short time. The spray, snow and sleet flying over the vessel and through the rigging quickly froze "until she looked like an iceberg." The barometer gave scant warning of the northwest blast until it struck, when it dropped 0.4 and then shortly rose to 29.60 inches.

The wind continued to blow with hurricane force with the crew battling to take in the foresail and fore-staysail, encased in ice. Only by the use of iron bars and sledge hammers were they able to get them half down where they were secured as best could be done on the heaving decks. Moving about was hazardous and the exposure extreme. Around 8 a.m. of the 12th, huge cross seas caused by the new northwest sea running into the old swell from the southeast, nearly overwhelmed the little schooner. The force of the driving sleet was so cutting that one could not look to windward, nor see the length of the vessel. Deprived of proper sail, the schooner would not lie hove-to, but lay broadside in the trough heading southwest. It became imperative to bring her head up. A drag was needed.

Their anchor pole, a heavy teak spar about 16 feet long by 5 inches in diameter, was rigged for this purpose with a kedge anchor and windglass bars lashed to it to provide weight. A riding hawser, made fast to a sling at the drag, was passed in through the hawse-pipe—a hero's job. Yet, it was all for nothing. Her head would not come up.

The crew next resorted to the use of oil. Three canvas bags were made, stuffed with oakum soaked in oil. One was put out forward, one 'midships, one on the weather quarter. The spreading oil reduced the force of the breaking seas. It was necessary to put iron bolts in the oil bags as the wind began to blow them out of the water and back aboard. The bags were filled with oil every half-hour by men crawling on deck with lifelines around them.

As the schooner still lay in the trough of the sea, it was decided to rig another drag. This time a heavier anchor was used with 65 fathoms of heavy rope, the stock being lashed to the shank to prevent its holding on the bottom. This device brought her head up and she rode with greater safety.

The schooner became so encased in ice that its weight was impairing her buoyancy and there was doubt whether she could survive the night. At 11:45 p.m., of March 12, she was struck by an unusually heavy sea and again thrown on her beam ends; everything moveable shifted to leeward; water poured down the fore hatch; she was close to foundering. Again, almost miraculously, despite the weight of ice, the splendid little vessel righted. There was no change in the wind force at midnight. Shrieking squalls, "as though they would lift her out of water," continued to rush over her.

At 5 a.m., the hawser of the sea anchor parted at the hawsepipe. The foresail could not be set as it was a solid mass of ice, so the storm trysail was broken out and helped to bring her head up.

Early in the morning of the 13th, the *Marshall* fouled the drifting mast of Pilot Boat No. 6, the *William H. Starbuck* and it was believed that she had foundered. They had no way of knowing that she had been in collision with a Japanese steamer, lost her mainmast, but happily survived. However, the *Phantom* and the *Enchantress* went down with all hands not far from them.

While the wind eased some after 4 p.m., the enormous weight of ice still endangered the vessel as seas swept the decks. About 6 p.m., they decided to risk it and wear around to the north; they made it, but nearly lost a man. Starting in the evening, it took over three hours to beat off enough ice to set some working sail and get the vessel under control. She had been driven 100 miles and more to the southeastward in 48 hours.

The morning of March 14 broke clear and moderate. After five hours more work, the sails and spars were reasonably clear of ice and they were standing to the westward under all sail. Throughout the storm the men had been in wet clothes; their faces and hands were badly frostbitten; they had had no food nor heat and were at the point of complete exhaustion.

Captain Partridge and Boat-keeper Robinson admirably met their responsibilities. They were not only skilful seamen but men of courage, and by their example kept hope in the others. Robinson stated that, "No man showed the slightest sign of fear, the feelings of each one known only to himself, but all trusting in Providence to pull her safely through."

The Highlands of New Jersey were sighted at nightfall. Normally when inbound ships converging on the entrance to New York Harbour, missed the off-shore cruising pilot schooners, there was always one on hand off Sandy Hook. Yet on March 14 the pilots of the *Marshall* found no one covering the bar station. Did they proceed into port for badly needed treatment, and recuperation? No, indeed. Not while there were ships arriving in need of pilots.

The end of the report simply states:

"At 4 a.m., March 15, resumed station off the bar."

A Reader of the Sky

ON THE night of November 26-27, 1898, the people of the New England coast were wakeful. Their world had gone berserk. The wind howled with a fury uncontrolled. The houses rocked, the trees writhed and roared in their torture, wires screamed in protest and ships battled to live.

The violence weakened as the day advanced. It was Sunday. The stunned inhabitants looked about them at the desolation of wreckage in every form. Communications were all but suspended, highways blocked with trees and wires, coastlines were changed, wrecks and wreckage strewed the beaches. At Plymouth the Eel River's mouth was relocated; on the beach 24 houses were gone; every schooner in the usually safe anchorage was ashore. All up and down the coast, cottages were upset and piazzas blown away. The North River's mouth was found to have moved two miles north and was located where houses were standing only 12 hours before; now there was a depth of six feet at low water. In the marshes, a mile inland, the railroad bed was gone. I saw the sleepers and rails like a great snow fence standing against the telegraph poles for support.

As the day passed, crippled ships began to make port. Seagoing tugs came in without their barges, some without their wheelhouse windows. Dismasted vessels were reported rolling helplessly on the sea. The steamer *Portland* was overdue at Portland; the *Pentagoet* (formerly the famous Coast Survey steamer *Bibb*)* last seen off Chatham has never since reported.

In those days, ferries, North and South, ran back and forth between Boston and East Boston, an island. Between them was an anchorage for one vessel, perhaps two. There laying safe and undamaged amidst all the vast destruction afloat, was the schooner *Lavinia Snow*. Of all the weatherwise skippers on Saturday November 26, hers was unsurpassed.

That Saturday was the most subtle weather breeder that ever seduced the New England coast. Indian summer came back to say goodbye; it was mild, a pleasant haze lay over land and sea. The barometer was reading 30.0 inches at noon; a low swell rolled on the sea with only a gentle breeze.

Amid these serene conditions a small harbour

*This vessel on hydrographic surveying duty in the combat zone of the Civil War received Gen. William T. Sherman as he reached the coast after his march through Georgia. The General and Admiral Dahlgren lunched and planned aboard the *Bibb*.

tug—I think she was the *Vesta*—was steaming out
to sea. An old friend, the late Lieutenant-Commander Denis McCarthy, on that distant day was
a deck hand aboard the tug and gave me the
thread of this episode of the great storm. He and
the other hand were sitting on the forward bitts
enjoying the sunshine; the engineer occasionally
came out of his engine-room, to sit on the rail and
appreciate the mild fresh air. The skipper leaned
on his forearms in the open wheelhouse window
sweeping the horizon for a sail, hoping that some
captain was anxious to spend Sunday in port rather
than lie offshore becalmed.

A large four-master in the distance led him
far beyond the range of his normal harbour duties,
even venturing to a point off Cape Cod, some 40
miles from Boston Light. She came up abreast the
big vessel, lying nearly becalmed with sails gently
thumping as she rolled easily to the low swell.
The crew lounged about as lazy and unruffled as the
vessel herself. Her master, too, showed an attitude
of not having a care in the world as he stood with
one foot on the low rail aft.

"Want a tow, Cap'n" shouted the *Vesta's*
skipper.

'No, Jim, I might as well be here as in the
Mystic. Tomorrow's Sunday." The captain's reasoning was sound enough from his point of view;
idly tied up to a wharf in the Mystic River was
hardly a better choice, unless the shore held attrac-
tions. Yet he had not the slightest hint that his

decision was the most momentous he had ever made.

The masters of all coastal vessels were always on an exposed lee shore with little sea room; of necessity they kept the changes of weather under their closest scrutiny. Not only their lives, but their property and their reputations depended upon their accuracy in reading precursory signs. This captain's mind, if judged by his bearing, was perfectly tranquil, no apprehensions were disturbing his thoughts.

The skipper of the *Vesta* responded, with the usual courtesy among sailors, by tossing the latest newspaper aboard the schooner and with a wave of the hand ringing up the engine. The presence of a three-master, a short distance to the southward, occupied his attention. Aboard her they soon saw a singularly contrasting scene, all was activity, seamen rushing about, while the master paced nervously near the wheel.

"Want a tow, Capn?"

"Yes, get me damn quick out of here," a reply that astonished the *Vesta's* people. They were perplexed by all the excitement in such fine weather. They were interested, however, for they were conscious that Vesta was a small low-freeboarded tug far from home.

Communications in those days were confined to land lines and at that very hour they were buzzing with warnings of trouble on the way. All those out on the sea were in ignorance, all but the

F

Portuguese skipper of the *Lavinia Snow*. What did he see that others failed to note?

It is believed now that he was a keen observer of the high cirrus and that he detected a suspicious cloud movement in the upper air that to him were the outriders of a furious storm. Unknown off Cape Cod was that the union of a low pressure coming up the coast and a depression from the west had taken place to the south. The result was a storm of great intensity rushing northward for the New England coast with unprecedented velocity.

The *Vesta* started her long, heavy tow. Soon the weather began to change, an easterly breeze, thickening overcast and rising sea. The wind increasing settled in the no'theast. It began to snow, the wind reaching a gale before tug and tow made the entrance to the harbour. The *Portland* passed them to her doom. After passing Boston Light the tug hauled up for the Narrows, bringing the wind abeam. The schooner was almost swept from her control. The valiant tug battled her way up the harbour yard by yard and hours later brought her charge to an anchorage "between the ferries." There, with two anchors down and a long scope of chain out, she rode precariously through that ferocious night, while scores of vessels were foundering, dismasting or being broken up on the wild ledges and beaches.

The greatest intensity of the storm prevailed between midnight and 6 a.m. As the tumult eased some hours later, people began to venture to the shores. The destruction was staggering. The searchers among the piles of wreckage, snow and ice, found bodies tangled with the fragments of their vessels. The crew of the *Lavinia Snow* must have thought deeply on their good fortune to have sailed with a genius in weather wisdom.

That big four-master with its placid crew of a few hours before, had no chance to claw off that rocky lee shore of Boston Harbour entrance. She was driven on the ledges by the fury of the wind and sea. All of her that could be identified amidst the chaos of sails, spars and timbers, was the quarter-board bearing her name.

Those in the *Vesta* could never forget her captain's fatal words as he declined their hawser:

"No, Jim, I might as well be here as in the Mystic."

PART III

Sea Turns

This term
applies to an abrupt
shift to a refreshing sea breeze.
Admittedly among these vignettes of the
experiences of certain sailors, there are some
that fall short of being refreshing, but at least
they will change the line of thought as the sea turn
alters the prevailing humidity.

Sea Turns

The Captain's Guest

Many years ago, perhaps up to the outbreak
of the First War, one might meet an officer of the
armed forces who was something less than enthusi-
astic concerning reservists and civilians, especially
when they intruded his precincts. And this regard-
less of their cultural stature. Happily this attitude
has gone by the board and for a long time a reserv-
ist has stood on his merits.

In this connection I recall an amusing incident which is a case in point. It came to me from
two independent and reliable sources. When I
joined the Hydrographic Office of the Navy in 1908
there was among the employees a gentleman so
decrepit his daughter was obliged to assist him to
work each morning. He was Major Bowles of the
Civil War, college educated and once a man of
parts. There was then no retirement in the Civil
Service so men worked as long as they could reach
their desks.

Shortly after his war service, Major Bowles,

then Mr. Bowles, as a hydrographic surveyor, was ordered to a ship surveying in the North Carolina Sounds. This vessel was officered by naval officers. Mr. Bowles reported aboard and presented his orders to the executive officer. After some brief, cool generalities, he asked to be shown to his quarters. The officer hesitated awkwardly, informing the new arrival that he would be quartered forward.

Taken aback, Mr. Bowles replied that there must be some misunderstanding—that the situation was not as had been represented to him upon appointment. The next step in the ordinary routine was to report his presence to the Captain. This officer was a highly respected and understanding gentleman. In the cabin Mr. Bowles was cordially greeted by, if my memory is accurate, Captain Rockwell.

As the complication was explained, the captain's countenance changed to incredulity. For a few moments he looked out the port in meditation. Then turning to Mr. Bowles with a whimsical smile, he said:

"It is lonely here by myself. It would be pleasant for me and I hope agreeable to you, to share my cabin and mess this winter."

So, no doubt, on occasion, the captain and Mr. Bowles could be seen discussing some favourite subject as they paced the starboard side of the quarter deck—the captain's side.

Lt. R. E. Byrd U.S.N. an Anecdote

It was after dinner of a summer's evening that I drove my car into the front tier of the parking lot overlooking the Duxbury yacht basin. A car pulled in alongside and Lieutenant Edward L. Gisburne U.S.N. (ret.), a medal of honour man, and I were soon deep in reminiscence. In this way I fathered a pleasant anecdote of Lieutenant (j.g.) Richard E. Byrd U.S.N.

Lieutenant Gisburne was a chief petty officer radio-man in the early days of this notable advance in communications. Then, four or five years before the First War it was new and somewhat mysterious, giving the radiomen a little more prestige than the regular ratings. At least through their work they were probably brought in closer touch with the officers.

The captain of the battleship in which C.P.O. Gisburne was serving, for some good reason of his own, ordered certain facilities shut down to conserve fuel. Among these was the cooling of the men's scuttlebutt (drinking fountain).

The day was hot and humid as Gisburne came out of his "shack" for a drink. The water was tepid. He expressed himself rather forcibly, not realizing that Lieutenant Byrd was standing directly above. A few minutes passed. An orderly came to the shack with the message that Lieutenant Byrd wanted to see him in his stateroom. Surprised at such a summons and questioning its import, Gisburne proceeded to the Lieutenant's room. He knocked. No answer. He opened the door a crack. No one there. He opened the door wide. On the desk was a large bowl of ice and buried in it was a bottle of ginger ale. He looked intently at this tempting refreshment: There was a card sticking in the bowl. It read:

"For Gisburne."

Land Ho!

It is interesting to see an insignificant act move on to play a part in a wider field. As an instance: An elderly lady scanning the death notices in her newspaper saw one that became the link in helping the State Department to establish the sovereignty of an island.

It was in 1936 that the National Geographic Society called the Hydrographic Office of the Navy asking for information regarding Heard Island in the far southern reaches of the Indian Ocean. The query came to my desk. The sailing directions of that region, through all editions, simply stated that the island was sighted by Captain Heard (otherwise unidentified) in the ship *Oriental* in 1853. The British directions carried the same information. I reported it back to the Society, but unofficially I wrote that I was intrigued by the question and on my own time would seek a more ample answer.

I sent a letter to my old friend Mrs. Ellen B. Stebbins, who had a pronounced slant for such puzzles. She had a deepwater seafaring background as well. I was advised to put an item in the "Query and Answer," column of the Boston Transcript— a valuable service in those days. This was done and there was no response. Mrs. Stebbins was disappointed. Only a few weeks passed and I received a letter from her with the bold opening sentence: "We are on the trail." Enclosed was the following death notice:

> JOHN REED HEARD, 80, formerly associated with Charles R. Thayer in the theatre ticket business in Boston, died suddenly in Los Angeles. Mr. Heard was a native of Boston, the son of Captain John J. Heard and Fidelia (Reed) Heard.

Among the surviving relatives mentioned was Dr. Mary A. Heard of Milton, Massachusetts, a sister. A letter to Dr. Heard brought a prompt reply:

> "The Captain Heard about whom you wish information was my father John Jay Heard. He sailed for Australia in August 1853."

The information developed that Matthew Fontaine Maury, the distinguished oceanographer, had requested Captain Heard to lay a course on this voyage along the great circle, between the Cape of Good Hope and Melbourne. It was to test its practicability in view of its shorter distance. It proved that this route took a ship too far south, in fact as far as Labrador is north in our hemisphere, and into the dangers of drifting Antarctic ice. Captain Heard sighted ice to the northward and southward of his course. This area is one with a high percentage of overcast and stormy skies.

By good fortune in 1853 on November 25, after passing snow squalls, the sky cleared for the *first time in 20 days* and Captain Heard was able to establish his position. About 8 a.m., in this clear interval, he sighted, to the northward, what appeared to be an iceberg, (They are as big as islands in those seas) but on closer approach proved to be land—an uncharted island. It was about 25 miles long by 11 miles wide and a peak 9,000 feet high, located in lat. 53° 12' S., lg. 73° 34' E.

The Captain strongly desired to land and place the flag on its shore, but the conditions were not favourable for that purpose and furthermore he was trying to make a fast passage on this test route.

This is an instance of the bold navigation of those hurrying days of the 1850's; running headlong under stormy skies for 20 days depending solely on dead reckoning; some 700 miles southward of the usual route; carrying light sails all night when possible; they split repeatedly, were sent down, repaired and bent again. On they drove despite icebergs in their path, difficult to see at night and in the snow, and then too, rising anxiety in passing patches of rock kelp with the haunting question, "Did it grow near here?"

A little apart from the discovery of an island is the fact that Mrs. Fidelia Heard accompanied her husband on this lonely voyage. Those seafaring women were truly hardy souls. She kept a detailed journal which is now in the possession of her grandson Joseph J. Heard.

Some four years after the letter from Dr. Heard, the Second War being on in Europe, each major country was seeking to establish sovereignty over long neglected islets and islands far and wide. Every atoll and projecting mountain top in the sea was being scrutinized and claimed. Bits of land that a year before had been devoid of interest, suddenly might be revealed to have potential value as a spot to land a plane.

About this time the State Department called on the Hydrographic Office for information concerning Heard Island. The query again came to me. So it came to pass that the sharp, though ageing eyes of Mrs. Ellen B. Stebbins caught the one-inch death notice to give us the opportunity of furnishing the full details for the official records.

Anything Can Happen in War Time

Early in 1943 my cousin, Horatio Phipps, like many another young man found himself aboard the crowded transport *Mount Vernon* heading for parts unknown. She sailed from San Diego passing unescorted through the South Pacific, on southward of Australia, stopping briefly at Melbourne, and northward in the Indian Ocean. Before reaching Australian waters they heard Tokyo Rose's propaganda broadcast on the public speaker system, sadly regretting the sinking of the *Mount Vernon*. Yet they arrived safely in Bombay.

Phipps was later selected for duty with cryptographic communications and his tour in Ceylon ran for two years. The tremendous power of the Japanese sweep through the East Indies and along the Asian coast had been halted and reversed. Singapore had been retaken.

It was necessary to quickly set up a signal centre in the Malayan city. At 10:30 p.m., Sergeant Jones and Corporal Phipps were given a half hour before leaving their beautiful headquarters in the Botanical Gardens near Kandy. Travelling by jeep through the dark night they arrived at a small fighter strip outside of Colombo at 2:00 a.m.

They reported to the British officer waiting for them at the gangway of a big special Lancaster plane.

"You mean, Sir, that we are to fly in this plane?" Phipps inquired incredulously. "Isn't it Admiral Mountbatten's plane?"

"Yes. It has been held two hours for you."

The officer escorted the two non-coms aboard the flag ship, turning them forward into a luxurious cabin; not aft down an aisle where colonels and two generals were seated. They were amazed at their importance—a new experience and as they said, "We loved it."

In the cabin running each side was a deep, soft, foam rubber cushion bed covered with rich, blue leather. The carpeted floor, two easy chairs, bureaus and mirrors all added to the comfort of travel in war time. Phipps slept in the starboard bunk—the one used by the Admiral. Up bright and early the next morning, Phipps opened a door and several British officers at breakfast, stood up. Evidently there was respect for anyone occupying that cabin, especially in *uniforms without distinguishing insignia.*

"At ease," suggested Phipps, relieving the situation. The soldiers were hospitably served a fine breakfast.

Phipps surveying his novel quarters, inspected the guest book, becoming impressed by the names who had shared his honour of riding the private plane of the Commander-in-chief of Southeast Asia, Admiral Lord Louis Mountbatten. In the distinguished list were the American generals: MacArthur, Eisenhower, Arnold, Wedermeyer, Stillwell and Sultan. Among many of England's top rank was Field Marshal Tedder of the Royal Air Force. This famous plane had transported officers of the highest echelon to the historic war time conferences of Churchill, Roosevelt and Stalin.

"Well, I'm a guest," mused Phipps, taking his pen, he inscribed:

"Horatio Phipps, Corporal, U.S. Army.*

*The plane landed at Singapore on a rain drenched runway on the heels of the Jap withdrawal. The two buddies, in record time, set up the South East Asia Command Signal Centre in the Governor's mansion.

An Exhumed Wreck

Early in December 1901, I was temporarily detached from the U.S. Coast Survey steamer *Enedavor* and ordered to Ocean City, New Jersey. I was to assist William Bowie, a distinguished officer of the Survey, in making an examination of the bar. We hired a boatman and launch equipped with an unreliable engine. It was very cold and the frozen bilge water added to the discomfort. Thirty years later, when on occasion, I met Major Bowie, he would invariably ask "Have you got warm yet, Bradford."

On the evening of December 14 the wind was blowing a gale and the thought came to me that these conditions might cause a shipwreck. With the wind whistling and the surf pounding, I went to sleep. In the night I was aroused by droning shouts in the street, "ship ashore," but thought I was dreaming. Later, I heard people running about the house, "There's a wreck on the beach." I quickly dressed, heading for the shore in the cold grey dawn.

To witness the wreck of a great sailing ship is a dismal and emotional experience. There she was, then broadside to the beach, seas breaking on the weather side and heavy spray breaching clear across the decks. Her topsails had been set when she struck, but now the sheets had parted and those immense sails were beating wildly in the high wind, with such great booming sounds that they could be heard a half-mile away, even above the

The Sindia

wind. The canvas soon gave way under such destructive power and became streaming ribbons
from the yards.

The vessel had been built as a steamer, by
Harland and Wolff of Belfast, Ireland, in 1887. In
1892 her engines were removed and she was rigged
as a four-masted bark. On July 8, 1901 she sailed
from Kobe, loaded with a miscellaneous cargo of
Japanese merchandise, bound for New York.

I arrived in time to see a boat come through
the surf; there was no loss of life. That is, not

G

directly. It was later reported that Captain McKenzie, before a British court of inquiry, lost his licence for six months. The humiliation and the disaster broke his spirit. With his fine reputation impaired, he returned to his native Scotland and shortly died.

His mistake evidently was in coming on the coast without the precaution of sounding, which in that locality, gives ample warning. However, taking a sounding in a sailing ship was an awkward operation and many a luckless master has put too much confidence in his estimated position.

The *Sindia* was never salvaged. She was slowly worked inshore by the sea and the moving sands gave way for her until, as the years passed, the great ship settled out of sight. Some years ago a friend sent me a post card that showed only a steel mast projecting from the beach and over her once sea-washed decks, decades of children have played in the summer's sun.

The catastrophic storm of March 1962, that ravaged the coast from New York to below Hatteras, changing shore-lines and depths, swept the sand from the buried *Sindia* and again exposed her decks to wind and salt spray.

Restraint

My friend Sargent White, during the last war, was in a plane heading for San Francisco on government business. Sitting beside him was a lieutenant j.g. who by his appearance and tarnished stripes had seen some heavy service. Their desultory conversation consisted of commonplace pleasantries.

Arriving in Nashville they were "bumped off" by more urgent and higher rank. They proceeded to the rendezvous in such circumstances, standing around in the hotel lobby waiting for the chance of a seat in a plane bound west.

A lieutenant-commander in bright new stripes and significantly wearing no campaign ribbons ostentatiously confronted the lieutenant.

"Why are you out of uniform in that blue shirt?" he demanded brusquely.

"It was unavoidable, Sir. I'll rectify it as soon as possible."

"See that you do," and the officer disappeared with the apparent satisfaction of having meticulously done his duty.

The lieutenant turned to White with a steely glint in his eye and a cool hard smile.

"I could have explained that I had arrived in New York from Europe only an hour before I took the plane and could have added that all my white shirts were lost when my mine-sweeper was sunk off the Anzio Beach-head.* But I didn't want to spoil his act."

1* .I have later learned that the lieutenant had finished sweeping the approaches to the beach-head, but with a little time before dawn he decided to make a final sweep as against some missed stray mine. It was a fatal decision; he was detected, the German 88's opened up and his vessel was sunk under him.

Christmas on the Underside

There was a high expectancy on the faces of the hurrying crowd. Everyone was heavily encumbered with packages of gifts. Despite age-weighted feet I still wanted to be a part of Christmas Eve if only for an hour. There is a singular enchantment in the colour, flashing lights, the splendour of the show windows, and the good will in the air. You seem to feel less a stranger on the street at Christmastime. The tinkling bell of the Salvation Army led me to the kettle where I dropped my tribute to conscience. The devoted, elderly little lady, with the off-face bonnet and red ribbons, looked up and smiled; I returned it with sincerity; it was my respect for her order. She gave us all an opportunity to square our extravagancies; she and her kettle are an important part of the Christmas pageant.

Late that evening, alone before a tired fire and with a freshly loaded pipe, I drifted into reveries, as so many do, of the Christmases I have known. Some have been bleak, many joyful, but there was one in 1907 that I shall never forget, not a detail, notwithstanding its distant date. There was a girl; she was something more than pretty. Her face will always remain imprinted on my mind, though I only observed her in pure admiration.

Shortly before beginning my duties in the Hydrographic Office, I did a stretch with the telephone company. My pleasant work was with the P.B.X's (private branch exchanges), but between those jobs I filled in on any other assignment. This was the situation on Christmas eve, or rather afternoon. The foreman had given me several, apparently easy, trouble-shooting calls. One of them turned out to be difficult, so, when I headed for the last address, it was getting dark; a dank evening with icy streets and dismal low overcast.

The place I sought proved to be a saloon located on the waterfront of the city. I pushed open the door of the long, narrow, crowded room, suddenly meeting a loud bedlam of argument, here and there moaning and sobs. I had been a sailor in years gone by and although notably temperate, waterfront bar-rooms were no novelty, but this was the worst I had ever seen. Tawdry chains of red and green paper swung radially from the central jets and MERRY CHRISTMAS in a white wash sprawled across the mirror behind the bar. The bar-keep seeing my tool kit nodded to the instrument on the wall midway opposite the bar.

One fellow had collapsed head and shoulders on the bar sobbing and yammering something about his Jenney, whether mother, wife or child, no one could tell had they paid any attention— which they did not. Two men near him talking, seriously even above the din, were the only coherent words in the place, but they were entirely oblivious to the man crumpled on the bar beside them. At the tables along the wall where I worked, men babbled in their schooners of beer; two pals at my elbow roared raucously at ribald jokes, all heedless of a prostrate man down among their feet and table legs. On the other side of me, an elderly fellow, who seemed to be a lone wolf, was slumped in his chair, with feet far extended. He was neat; there were clear tracings of intelligence in his face as he looked intently at the floor. Clutching his glass, he gave the appearance of trying to push down and drown all thoughts of Christmasses past.

The air of the room was thick and foul; the usual rather pleasant malty smell of a bar-room, mixed with the fragrance of live tobacco, degenerated here into a stench composed by honest, yet aged, sweat revived by the heat, long extinguished cigar butts and sour alcoholic breaths.

Poor fellows, they were largely industrious workers plodding through long-houred days for a scanty wage. This was all that Christmas was bringing them; the slow awakening tomorrow would precede a remorseful and painful holiday.

Suddenly the door opened, quickly followed by three loud commanding raps on a tambourine. An unbelievable hush swept the room as though the muddle headed men had heard the voice of the Lord. There stood a young, petite Salvation lass. Through the veil of smoke her lovely features with off-face bonnet held by its red ribbons, appeared singularly delicate amid the grossness about her. What a place for a pretty unattended girl! How meticulous must have been the behaviour of those girls to command such impressive respect from these unshaven, frowsy men of the lower tiers of humanity!

The lass was either remarkably astute or had been carefully trained, for she remained standing at the entrance for a few seconds with eyes directly ahead just as one would expect of a determined angel. This delay, quite apparently, was calculated to allow dirty hands to grope in shallow pockets for a nickel or a dime. She did not intend to pause, once she entered their midst. Rapidly the girl glided down the line of men at the bar, small coins gently thudding on the stretched vellum of the tamborine —the only sounds in the strange stillness. The barkeeper reached over, perhaps on the house, dropped a coin with a noticeable thump. As I remember, she did not even say, "Thank you," utter silence was probably a subtle point in her technique, used under the circumstances. Yet there was no danger, for in that crowd there were enough men who would not have allowed even a touch on that girl's arm.

In that collection there was more than a handful of coins; she had taken the next drink from their very lips, and as it were, put it to their credit for the privilege of a bath, a bowl of soup and a cot on some dead-end night.

The man with out-stretched legs beside me, drew them in as she passed, dropping a quarter and appeared to feel better for it. Then from the still hushed room she vanished through the door like a blue phantom—from Samaria.

Christmas, Another Side

There are some of us who used to follow the shipping arrivals at Boston still remember the frequent item: "Arrived: Tug Lehigh, McGoldrick, with barges from Philadelphia."

Navigating our rugged coastal waters for over 50 winters had toughened every fibre in the being of Michael McGoldrick, except his tender heart. As master of the *Lehigh* he carried heavy burdens when the bulk of New England's coal was brought from the south outside around Cape Cod. He, of necessity kept a vital schedule with the weather. There were then no radio broadcasts. The number of lives in his charge was not large, but they were in a vulnerable position—in the deeply-laden barges astern. Their lives were dependent upon the weather wisdom of the tug master, when he pushed out by Chatham in the winter time. At five knots he had to forecast conditions 8 to 10 hours ahead, for there was no shelter short of Provincetown. With such demands on the sea-going tug masters, Captain McGoldrick was a notable instance of longevity and who never lost a life or a vessel.

A tug captain was best judged by those who served in the barges. They respected Michael McGoldrick for his character, for his unusual ability and he was loved for his sympathetic nature. This appraisal came to me from an official of his company who in his youth was a hand in the barges the captain towed astern.

Captain McGoldrick also had a well-ballasted mind for he sustained unbalancing family losses in his latter days: His wife died, closely followed by his eldest son, lost at sea with all hands, the next son, master of a sailing vessel foundered with all hands, the youngest son, in a government vessel was lost off the coast. Bracing himself against these shocks the old man continued to navigate his *Lehigh* until 81 years of age.

After his retirement had you stood on a certain street corner at Christmas time in Perth Amboy, you might have seen an elderly, but active, man surrounded by a large group of children, laughing and chattering as they trotted along about him. They were rather shabbily dressed, but their clothes were the best they had. The man entered the door of the neighbourhood hotel and the youngsters crowded in excitedly.

There in a brightly lighted room was a large, gaily decorated table, with mounds of fruit, dishes of goodies and a bag of candy at each place. The octogenarian, Captain Michael McGoldrick, seated himself at the head of the table; the children with dancing eyes wiggled into the nearest chairs. A large Negro, with a wide smile, stood in the doorway holding a platter upon which rested a big brown turkey. This capped the makings of a great feast. Youthful ecstasy reigned noisily. The ancient mariner was having Christmas too.

Skill When Needed

A group of officers during the late war, were standing on the after deck of a beaten-up carrier out in the Pacific. She was about to be sent back to a home base for extensive repairs. An admiral (from whom I picked up this incident) of the staff of C in C, Pacific, was making the decisions. A relief carrier had arrived at this advanced base, but had been obliged to sail for the war area without a radar antenna—that "bedspring" we used to see on naval vessels. It was decided to send down the antenna of the damaged carrier and transfer it to the new arrival so much in need of it.

The executive officer ordered the plan put into operation. In a short time the officer-of-the-deck came aft with the surprising announcement that there was no bo's'n in the ship who could perform this piece of seamanship. The officers looked at each other with undisguised dismay, somebody muttering that seamanship had gone to hell.

At this juncture a junior officer brought word that an enlisted man had declared that he could do the job. In our ships it seems that there is always someone to do the task at hand. The captain ordered that the man be brought aft. The blue-jacket reiterated his confidence. The colloquy ran something like this:

"What equipment would you need?"

"A length of water pipe, a short piece of rope and a lowering tackle, Sir."

"You will need more gear than that."

"I think not, Sir."

"What experience have you had to undertake this? That equipment is very valuable right now."

"I am a steeplejack, Sir."

Springs Are Where You Find Them

At sea when some disablement occurs the officers and crew are faced with a challenge to their ingenuity. It frequently happened in sailing vessels, but occasionally in power propulsion the engineers, and sometimes the deck officers, are called upon to use their wits.

An old friend served as the engineering officer in a submarine shortly after the First War. They were bringing her home across the Atlantic when obliged to work themselves out of a serious dilemma. Still far from New York the valve's compression springs of the diesel motor began to break. With each failure a cylinder was put out of action.

After all the spares had been used, the engineers were on their own resources. It was an opportunity for any one with an idea to speak up. Someone suggested that there were springs in his mattress. This at another time might have appeared humorous as there seemed to be little in common between mattress and engine springs. However, they were springs and springs can serve two purposes.

It was reasoned that if the bed springs were secured to the overhead, above the engine, they could serve as tension springs and do the work of the broken compression springs. The valves would be lifted instead of being pushed up normally. The exercise of ingenuity brought the desired results.

As more springs failed more of the mattress was demolished. At length nearly all the original springs had carried away. In due course, more or or less on schedule, the submarine passed through the Narrows of New York, hitting on every cylinder, with a labyrinth of dancing bed springs over the motor.

The Creeping Mists

Zeke and Cy, the old boatman and the retired sea captain, had bragged throughout their long lives on their keen eyesight. Now in their twilight years they were obliged to give some ground and they did it reluctantly. Although their frequent fishing trips were in Zeke's boat, Cy, through long habit, dominated every move. Zeke was tolerant.

One day in the late fall news came that there were large codfish off the Gurnet. This report lured Zeke and Cy to brave the cold discomforts for some prize fish.

Also at that time of year there were many ducks working southward for better feeding grounds. Among those that frequented local waters were whistlers and quandies.* They have both dark

*The quandy is also and perhaps better known as the old squaw duck; sometimes it is called a "sou' southerly", owing to its quack having a resemblance in sound to south-southerly. The whistler is a golden-eye duck.

and white markings requiring some discernment at a distance.

The two fishermen were returning from an early morning try at the codfish. They were sailing slowly up the channel with a light easterly breeze.

"There's a quandy up ahead," Zeke observed mildly.

"It's a whistler," promptly contradicted Cy. "You are getting decrepid. Your legs are giving out and now your eyes are going."

"Just because you have squinted at a lot of blue water doesn't mean you can tell a whistler from a quandy. It's a quandy."

"Betcha a bucket of clams," shouted Cy.

"Take ya, and when you bring the clams to the house, Maggie will say, 'Good of ya Cy, come to dinner and have a nice chowder.'"

"No chowder, 'cause it's a whistler."

The boat sailed slowly towards the bird. It did not dive, nor did it fly. Suddenly there fell a deep silence in the boat. A neatly painted black and white lobsterpot buoy was slowly passing by.

Cuisine to Order

Abner Starfish had lobstered and fished for 30 years and thought he had had enough of cold, rough weather. He longed for a living ashore. As he was getting along in years this was not easy.

However, there was an idea rolling around in his mind. Molly, his wife, was an excellent cook and why not capitalise on her gift! The happy part of that was, she would do anything to get him out of that boat.

So they found a building close to the harbour, took a lease and opened a sea food spot and were in business. They specialized in clams and lobsters. Over the fireplace Abner hung a sign, "Say how you want 'em, you get it."

Early one evening a big car drove up and a fashionably dressed couple went in. Abner showed them to a table. Steamed clams were ordered.

"Molly, two steams," Abner called down the dumb waiter.

The lady beckoned to Abner:

"I dislike that black material in the round part of the clams. Could that be removed?"

The sign said, "Say how you want 'em," so Abner proceeded to make good.

"Molly, those steams? Squart the bellies out of them clams."

Penitential Revenge

Captain Amasa Weatherell left his widow with a small competence. She was a good manager and could make out by strict economies. Her better-off relatives were critical of all she did and humbled her on many occasions. At length she decided to have her revenge. She sold her house with the pretence of boarding around. Soon her relatives and friends were shocked to learn that she had been admitted to board in the poor house! A cousin calling on her demanded:

"Why, under the sun Amantha, did you come to this place? You are embarrassing us to death."

"Good, that's just what I am here for."

Leave her, Johnny

In the days of our fathers and grandfathers there was a popular sea shanty among seamen that was called "Leave her, Johnny, leave her." There were two sets of words, with endless variations, for the tune: One, used at the pumps when the ship was leaking, suggesting it was time to leave her. But the other set of words, more appropriate at the moment, were used when the ship was finishing her voyage. Should your grandfather have been standing on the pier-head when a new arrival was being tied up in her berth, he might have heard the seamen pulling on a line in rhythm to the song:

O, the times are hard and the wages low,
I guess it's time for us to go.
    Leave her, Johnny, leave her.
Didn't I hear the bo's'n say,
One more pull and then belay?
    Leave her, Johnny, leave her.
I'm sure I heard the Old Man say,
Now go ashore and get your pay.
    Leave her, Johnny, leave her.